ANG

CELESTIA

OF THE

KHMER EMPIRE

PHOTOGRAPHS BY JON ORTNER

TEXT BY IAN MABBETT,
ELEANOR MANNIKKA, JON ORTNER,
JOHN SANDAY, AND JAMES GOODMAN
AFTERWORD BY KERYA CHAU SUN

The Khmer temples at Angkor are the world's most astonishing architectural treasure. Built between the ninth and the thirteenth centuries by a succession of twelve Khmer kings, Angkor spreads over 120 square miles (312 sq. km) in Southeast Asia and includes scores of major architectural sites. In 802, when construction began on the first temple in the Angkor area, with wealth from rice and trade, Jayavarman II took the throne, initiating an unparalleled period of artistic and architectural achievement, exemplified in the fabled ruins of Angkor, center of the ancient empire. Among the amazing pyramid- and mandala-shaped shrines preserved in the jungles of Cambodia, is Angkor Wat, the world's largest temple, an extraordinarily complex structure filled with iconographic detail and religious symbolism. Perhaps because of the decline of agricultural productivity and the expansion of the Thai Empire, Angkor was abandoned in the fifteenth century and left to the ravages of time. Today, many countries continue efforts to conserve and restore the temples, which have been inaccessible until recently. Now that the civil war has ended, Angkor is being reborn and is an increasingly popular tourist destination.

In this exquisitely illustrated book Jon Ortner has photographed fifty of the most important and unique monuments of the Khmer Empire. In additional to Angkor Wat his portrayal includes the miniature beauty of Banteay Srei; the elegant Preah Vihear, majestically located on the edge of a cliff; Bayon, whose towers are carved with over two hundred colossal faces; the newly restored Royal Terrace at Angkor Thom; and the roman tic temple of Ta Prohm partially engulfed by the jungle. His images include spectacular views from the rooftops of its temples, glorious landscapes, and details of basreliefs and rare art that few have ever seen.

The text by a team of distinguished experts provides up-to-date historical, architectural, and religious analyses of Angkor and the Khmer civilization. The Appendix offers a glossary and a chronology of Khmer kings and their accomplishments. Black-and-white floor plans and historic watercolors complete this breathtaking tribute.

ANGKOR

CELESTIAL TEMPLES
OF THE
KHMER EMPIRE

ANGKOR

CELESTIAL TEMPLES

OF THE

KHMER EMPIRE

PHOTOGRAPHS BY
JON ORTNER

TEXT BY IAN MABBETT, ELEANOR MANNIKKA,
JON ORTNER, JOHN SANDAY, AND JAMES GOODMAN
AFTERWORD BY KERYA CHAU SUN

ABBEVILLE PRESS PUBLISHERS
NEW YORK ~ LONDON

CONTENTS

THE
CENTRAL ANGKOR AREA

THE TEMPLES
SURROUNDING ANGKOR

THE
OUTLYING TEMPLES

INTRODUCTION

Jon Ortner

As the plane rose from Phnom Penh, headed for Siem Reap in northwestern Cambodia, flooded rice fields unfolded beneath us in all directions; a shimmering patchwork reflected the sun as it broke through the leaden monsoon clouds. Paddies alternated with verdant forests in an emerald mosaic. Eventually the vast tapestry ended; we had come upon the flooded shores of Tonle Sap, the largest lake in Southeast Asia, and the most productive freshwater fishery in the world. This inland sea, its surface swept by waves, tides, and violent storms, is the geographic and historic heart of the Khmer empire. The lake and its connection to the Mekong River created the abundance of natural resources that supported one of the most majestic and artistically expressive civilizations ever to rise on Earth, the Khmer.

Cambodia remains one of the least known and most mysterious countries in Asia. It is the remnant of a great Khmer empire, which at its zenith stretched from the coast of Vietnam to Bagan in Myanmar, including much of what is today Thailand. Between the ninth and thirteenth centuries, twelve Khmer kings built a succession of royal capitals in this forbidding region. The crowning achievements of these cities were hundreds of gargantuan temples, unmatched in their fusion of art, architecture, and philosophy. The royal families were said to have descended from the union of two legendary divine lineages, one solar, one lunar, and so the kings of the Khmer became living gods and the temples their divine inspirations.

Each spring brings a thaw to Himalayan glaciers thousands of miles away, and there, high upon the Tibetan plateau, the Mekong River is born. Flowing down through China, Myanmar, Laos, and into Cambodia, these glacial waters combine with the prodigious rains of the monsoon. From June to October the Mekong overflows its banks, bringing water and fertile red silt to a huge basin that has been home to the Khmer and their ancestors for millennia. As the Mekong floods, one of its main tributaries, the Tonle Sap River, also floods and reverses its flow, backing up and emptying into the Tonle Sap Lake. Astoundingly, each year the lake more than triples in size to encompass fully one-seventh of Cambodia's total area. When the monsoon rains diminish, the great lake shrinks back to its original size. It is this ebb and flow of the waters, in seasonal harmony with the movements of the sun, the moon, and the stars, that the Khmer understood and worshiped, incorporating their advanced astronomical knowledge, combined with Hindu mythology, into the elegant geometric designs of the Angkor temples. Since the Khmer knew that numbers were an expression of the structure of the universe, Angkor was designed to function in mathematical and ritual harmony with that universe.

Just as the annual flooding of the Nile was pivotal to the power and success of the Egyptians, so it was this same cycle of flood and drought, of sowing and harvesting, that the ancient Khmer mastered. The Khmer were initially an upland people, living in the forest and worshiping the animistic deities of nature—the *neak ta*, the ancestor spirits, which are still worshiped to this day, along with Krong Peali, the serpent deity, owner of the land and controller of all forms of water. Angkor was carved from that dark, untamed, spirit-inhabited forest. Over centuries, the Khmer modified their environment, and Angkor became the center of a hugely productive agricultural area that depended upon mastery of water storage and irrigation. It is widely accepted that the Khmer farmers were successful in extending the growing season, perfecting the cultivation of many types of wild rice, including a type of floating rice that grows elongated stems to keep up with the rising and falling floodwaters. Their expert use of reservoirs, canals, dikes, and water wheels created a productive rice economy capable of feeding the more than 1 million inhabitants of Angkor, the largest metropolitan area of the twelfth century. The aromatic woods, spices, and medicinal herbs of the tropical forests, the almost unlimited fish resources of the Tonle Sap Lake, and the agricultural fertility of the Mekong River basin created a confluence of physical and spiritual resources, a geographical imperative that for many centuries was the driving force behind the massive building projects of the Khmer kings.

On that same flight from Phnom Penh, looking down upon the stunning beauty of the countryside, I was momentarily transported back to my childhood. I could not have been much more than ten or eleven years old when I first saw the important and beautiful book *Angkor*, by Bernard-Philippe Groslier, who worked in Cambodia from 1959 through 1986, the son of the great French conservator Georges Groslier. Over the course of a distinguished career the elder Groslier had loved and protected the artistic and architectural heritage of the Khmer civilization. In 1916 he designed and created Cambodia's National Museum, which was to become a sanctuary for irreplaceable Khmer artwork during the many troubled times to come. I still cherish the images in that book. They had a profound effect on me—wonderful, richly toned black-and-white photographs of imposing temples, evocative scenes of gigantic monuments carved in stone, many of them imprisoned by the serpentine roots of huge trees. There, staring out from entangled vines, the huge faces of the Khmer rendered mute tribute to a fallen empire. Angkor was a dreamlike apparition, a lost city waiting to be explored. The specter of this legendary civilization and its god-kings calls out to us from a distant place lost in time. Angkor is that mystical place of imagination, perhaps more so than any other place on Earth. When the great naturalist and explorer Henri Mouhot first arrived at Angkor in 1860, he asked local people who had made these enormous monuments. They replied that they were the "work of giants," or that the "king of the angels" had built them. The glory of the temples was so great that even in their ruined state, their construction seemed beyond the capability of mortal humans. But in fact the richly endowed temples of Angkor were built by humans, vast armies of architects, artisans, and stonecutters, the ancestors of the people who live there now. Angkor is the sacramental creation of the most brilliant civilization to evolve in Southeast Asia.

As our flight continued across the Tonle Sap Lake, the spires of Angkor Wat appeared suddenly, thrusting high above the forest canopy, a temple mountain with five great stone peaks. Here is the greatest masterpiece of Khmer architecture, a magnificent shrine to the Hindu god Vishnu. Built at the end of the twelfth century, it required thirty-seven years to construct, and incorporates more stone than the pyramid of Kafre. Its moat and enclosure wall encompass nearly five-hundred acres, making it the largest religious building in the world. The funereal reliquary of the god-king Suryavarman II, it is seen by many scholars as the most perfect architectural monument ever created.

After the death of Jayavarman VII in 1218, Angkor went into a slow decline and was eventually sacked by the armies of Thailand around 1431. Although a steady trickle of Buddhist monks and pilgrims came to pray at the temple of Angkor Wat, the rest of the vast site was abandoned. Thousands of secular and religious buildings were left to the ravages of time and the engulfing tropical forest, and unknown quantities of art treasures were plundered. Except for a fifty-year period in the mid-sixteenth century, when the glories of Angkor were again briefly restored, the suffocating mantle of vine, moss, and root silenced and obscured the monuments once more. It was in this jungle-cloaked state that the first Westerners rediscovered the imposing ruins.

Even after five centuries of abuse and neglect, Angkor continues to instill amazement, wonder, and surprise—amazement at its size, its grandeur, and its mathematical exactness; wonder at its beauty and complex religious symbolism; and surprise as every turn reveals walls and towers covered with superbly crafted decoration. Designed to function ritually as earthly models of the cosmos, the temples of Angkor constantly remind us that we have entered the sacred universe, the dwelling place of the gods.

Most of what we know about the daily lives of the Khmer, and of the opulence of the Khmer temples and courts, comes from the writings of outsiders. One in particular, the Chinese emissary Chou Ta-kuan, lived at Angkor for one year, from 1296 to 1297. His detailed descriptions of daily life, the exceptional beauty of Khmer women, and the lavish ceremonies of the court give us a firsthand view of the riches of Khmer royalty. Inscriptions found at some of the temples detail the exact wealth and number of attendants used in their functioning. Thousands of villages with tens of thousands of inhabitants were needed to maintain a single temple and the daily rituals performed there. The treasuries were enormous, containing diamonds, pearls, gems, silks, gold, and all manner of other precious objects.

Over the years I have been privileged to examine and photograph these masterpieces of temple architecture at considerable length, studying the intricately decorated, miniature beauty of Banteay Srei, and the elegant Preah Vihear, majestically located on the edge of a sheer cliff on the Dangkrek escarpment. I have smelled the heavy perfume of jasmine and frangipani planted centuries ago by the Khmer. I have walked through the dripping forests at sunrise and heard the surreal ringing of cicadas and the screech of parrots in the canopy above Ta Phrom. I have been silenced and awed by the huge walls of Beng Mealea, so eloquently disappearing into the dense forest. I have looked into the faces of the Khmer kings and their celestial consorts, the *apsaras*, their dance forever frozen in stone. And as I have worked with and dwelled among these deepest emanations of man's search for a sacred context, I have developed a most profound respect for the ancient Hindu and Buddhist philosophies that inspired them.

The story of the construction, ascension, abandonment, and rediscovery of Angkor is the story of the Khmer civilization. Today, it elevates Angkor to its rightful position as one of the world's great architectural sites. All who love Angkor are part of this history, but we stand on the shoulders of intellectual luminaries—the researchers, conservationists, and scholars who dedicated their lives to the study and reconstruction of Angkor and in the process began to unlock the secrets of the Khmer civilization. What we have saved has been saved by their efforts; what we know, we know through the insights of scholars such as Louis Delaporte, Georges Coedès, Henri Parmentier, George and Bernard-Philippe Groslier, and the discoveries of explorers such as Henri Mouhot, Ernest Doudart de Lagrée, and Francis Garnier. And it was the first extensive photographic coverage of Angkor by John Thompson, fellow of the Royal Geographic Society in London, that brought the wonders of Cambodia to a truly worldwide audience.

Since 1907 the French, the Americans, and many other scholarly, philanthropic, and government organizations have worked tirelessly for the conservation and restoration of Angkor. More than a hundred years have been spent carefully rebuilding and protecting Angkor's monuments and religious art. In 1974 conservators were forced to leave because of the unspeakable destruction of life and property being visited upon the country by the Cambodian civil war. It was feared that the war would irreparably damage Angkor, or even destroy it, but miraculously the shrines have survived. The real threat comes as it always has, from theft, weather, and the rampant growth of tropical vegetation. Angkor was nominated as an UNESCO World Heritage Site in 1972 in recognition of its global cultural importance. Angkor's Khmer art and architecture are an expression of the most venerable philosophies in Asia—an encyclopedic storehouse of Hindu and Buddhist iconography.

This book is the culmination of my own passion and reverence for Angkor and the Cambodian people. Just as the photographs and text of Bernard-Philippe Groslier's volume enthralled me, I hope my photographs will now encourage a new generation of scholars, artists, and adventurers to continue the great work of understanding and protecting Angkor. To help me achieve this objective, I have asked five expert colleagues, each the best in his or her field, to write the text to complement my images, so that we might present an authoritative point of view concerning some of the newest and most provocative research being done at Angkor today.

John Sanday, noted restoration architect, who has directed the World Monuments Fund project at Preah Khan since 1989, writes on architecture and conservation. Ian Mabbett, leading expert on Khmer history, religion, and cosmology, shares his wisdom on those topics. Additional sections of text on hydrology by James Goodman and on the calendrical significance of Angkor Wat by Eleanor Mannikka are included. Kerya Chau Sun writes eloquently about the goals of APSARA and the future of Angkor.

The photographs lead the reader on an intimate exploration of fifty of the most important and unique monuments of the Khmer. More than thirty of these are richly decorated and highly symbolic temples. Beginning with the centerpiece of their civilization, Angkor Wat and the royal city of Angkor Thom, we examine the many surrounding temples, then move outward into the countryside, ending with the most remote temples along the Thai-Cambodian border, magnificently situated shrines at the farthest reaches of the Khmer empire.

In many ways, the work at Angkor is still young. Hundreds of sites throughout Cambodia remain to be identified, studied, protected, and restored. Our understanding of the importance and value of the Khmer culture continues to emerge. A new generation of Cambodian archeologists, preservationists, and scholars is being trained to continue the research and restoration that Angkor and the other sites require.

Angkor has bequeathed Cambodia and the world a lasting legacy and provides a focal point for the rebirth and flowering of Khmer culture. The sophisticated knowledge of the ancient Khmer, especially concerning rice cultivation and monsoon hydrology, is of great importance for the future of Cambodia and the whole of Southeast Asia. Carefully planned growth of tourism will help fuel the resurgence of Khmer traditional arts and fund both the continuing restoration efforts and the rebuilding of the Cambodian economy. Our overriding challenge now is to seek a balance between the legitimate needs of an emerging modern Cambodia and the resurrection of the temples of Angkor as living, sacred shrines.

ANGKOR:

HISTORY, RELIGION, AND CULTURE

Ian Mabbett

S ome people have little interest in ruins, or museums, or old places deliberately preserved like museum displays. They would not expect to enjoy a prolonged visit to Angkor. For them it holds no magic. These ruins, they think, cannot bring the past alive; the stone vestiges of an ancient city are inert, mute, part of a lost world that can no longer be entered or understood.

Of course, these people may well be convinced otherwise by this volume, but perhaps we should pause to consider how far the world of Angkor is really lost to us. Its remains consist of more or less ruined stone monuments, and of inscriptions in Old Khmer and Sanskrit on stone. The wooden buildings where people lived (including the palaces of kings) have all perished; only the stone structures have survived, nearly all representing religious foundations endowed by the great men of the land. These fragments of an antique civilization have lost the entire context in which they functioned. In the absence of this context, what meaning can they have for us?

One argument is convincing: the mood elicited in us as we survey the tumbled stone ruins is far from the spirit of Angkor as it originally was. Bats own the dark sanctuaries where gods once ruled, and aerial roots of strangler fig trees embrace crumbling towers. At the eastern gate of the Ta Som, a great tree twines itself around the fabric of the porch, gently prising apart the ancient stones. At Beng Mealea, at the eastern end of the Kulen Hills, the temple walls retreat into the lush green vegetation, camouflaged by thick vines and dense foliage. The atmosphere is romantic, melancholy. But the business of life in Angkor was not romantic. It was earnest and rational. Everything about the original design of the monuments, and of the cities that surrounded them, was governed by the quest for precision. Angkor was a machine; it would function only if the divine order of the heavens was properly encoded in the actions of kings and the conduct of rituals. Within the existing state of knowledge, priests and craftsmen were practical and logical.

This point is vital to understanding the reality of Angkor. Perhaps the bullet holes that pock the walls of the Phnom Bakheng sanctuary, a tactical hilltop stronghold in recent fighting, make a better symbol of life in Angkor—serious and often violent—than toppled stones asleep in the embrace of vegetation. But the religious monuments sponsored by rulers and court dignitaries, and the proud claims these leaders made in inscriptions, are arguably alien to the real life of ordinary people; they are therefore of very limited value for us as we try to come to grips with Cambodian history.

If this is so, how can we hope to comprehend the remains that lie before us now? We are confronted by two Angkors: the physical one, present in weathered blocks of stone, and the historical reality of the society that dwelled there, which now consists of shadows and distorted memories. No secure bridge connects the two. The truth about the real-life history of Angkor's

Opposite: Ink and watercolor illustrations of Angkor by Lucien Fournereau from an exhibition at the Paris Salon in 1889.

Relevé et dessiné par l'architecte imaginaire
PARIS. Mars 187.

people can be grasped, if at all, only after grappling with the riddles posed by the evidence.

Modern scholarship on the history of the region is not much more than a century old. Cambodia formed part of the French colonial territory in Southeast Asia (made a protectorate in 1863), and the chief home for modern research in this area was the Ecole Française d'Extrême-Orient (EFEO), founded at the end of the nineteenth century. No reliable documents record the ancient history of Cambodia, and research had to take the form of laborious detective work, piecing together the evidence from the inscriptions discovered, often in forgotten places amid ruins. This is not to say that the Khmers had abandoned and forgotten the past of Angkor's ancient sites—that is a common misconception—but they gave no ready answers to the questions of Western scholars.

Pioneering work was done by the scholars attached to the EFEO. Most notably, as far as Cambodia is concerned, Georges Coedès between 1904 and 1964 edited and translated all the inscriptions of Cambodia then known (others have been found and published since), combining this evidence with that of linguistics and foreign accounts to make the most connected possible story. Much of this work was necessarily speculative, and more recent work has rejected many of Coedès's interpretations. Nevertheless, he and his contemporaries in the EFEO laid the foundations of Cambodian studies.

After Cambodian independence, the EFEO continued to operate, but under increasingly difficult conditions. In the years since Pol Pot's regime, active study of Cambodia's past, archaeological as well as historical, has picked up momentum, actively nurtured by the Angkor Conservancy and the involvement of UNESCO in the preservation of Angkor, as well as by the research of scholars in France and elsewhere. Among French scholars, Claude Jacques has been particularly active, editing and translating new inscriptions, reexamining past research, and advancing fresh hypotheses. Many scholars in other countries have become involved in the ongoing quest to advance our knowledge. The field is wide open to new ideas and approaches, and the old certainties are all liable to be upset by new interpretations of the evidence. Ancient writings did exist on palm leaves and on deerskin, but these materials have all perished, and archives, where preserved, were eventually destroyed. The scantiness of evidence, for history and prehistory alike, has meant that the strength and distinctive qualities of civilization in Cambodia, and in the whole of Southeast Asia, have been slow to gain recognition. The earliest generations of scholars studying the history of Southeast Asia found it natural to treat the region as a passive recipient of more advanced culture brought in from outside. On this view, history began with the arrival of Indians, with their more advanced civilization, in the first two centuries A.D.

Since the 1970s and 1980s, however, it has become clear that Southeast Asia was never a backwater of civilization. On the contrary, its culture was well developed even in prehistoric times. One feature of this prehistoric culture was long-distance seafaring; from some early period, Southeast Asian sailors were able to cross the Indian Ocean to Africa. Another is the famous Dongson bronze culture (named after a site in Vietnam), which spread across much of Southeast Asia from about 600 B.C., leaving us the famous big ritual drums with incised patterns on their top surfaces, over two hundred of which have been found. A third is the construction of large forts, generally circular and surrounded by moats and embankments, in the period from about 400 B.C. to A.D. 300. In Cambodia, near tributaries of the Mekong and the Tonle Sap Rivers, these forts are witness to the organization of manpower, presumably by local chieftains, precursors of the kings who later arose. This civilization did not need the Indians to show it how to create political authority.

Various prehistoric Cambodian sites have been surveyed, and a few systematically excavated. Perhaps the most important is at Leang Spaan, where occupation has been recognized from about 6800 B.C. to late in the first millennium A.D. This of course overlaps with the historical period. The beginnings of history, as defined by the use of written records available to the historian, cannot be neatly dated for the Khmer country. The earliest local written records are inscriptions, the recording of which began only in the fifth and sixth centuries. However, organized states, with cities and advanced cultural forms, including writing, had at that time already existed for a while, and what we know about them comes in part from archaeology.

At an important site from the historical period, near where the Mekong River meets the sea, at Oc Eo, excavations conducted by Louis Malleret in the 1940s unearthed traces of a port city, linked to its hinterland by a network of canals. Artifacts found there include Indian objects, especially Buddhist ones—a bronze Buddha head, and a number of amulets with gold leaf—along with a miscellany of items dating from the first few centuries A.D.

Such sites were at first viewed as beachheads for Indian colonization, but nowhere is there any sign of Indian conquest or substantial immigration. It is more likely that most of the Indians who came were traders in settlements near the coasts. Adventurers and fortune seekers may have also ventured inland in search of gold and entered into relationships with local chieftains, perhaps intermarrying. Intermarriage, though, produced no visible effect upon the racial constitution of the population.

Archaeologists incline nowadays to date the beginnings of Indian contact with Southeast Asia to before, even well before, the beginning of the Christian Era. Beads, seals, coins, an ivory comb, and quantities of ceramics mark the presence of visitors from the West over a period of several centuries. Buddhist artifacts such as wooden images show that the priestly brahmanical orthodoxy did not have the running to itself. By the second century A.D., there was busy commercial activity, by all accounts, in Southeast Asian centers such as Oc Eo, where it appears likely that high-quality beads were manufactured for far-flung markets including China; the technology, it has been suggested, was the preserve of Tamils from India.

We know very little about the nature of the society to which the Oc Eo settlement belonged. A little, however, can be learned from Chinese dynastic histories. If we believe what we read, in the area of Cambodia a powerful state, called Funan by the Chinese, built up a substantial empire, extending its dominion around the Gulf of Siam and some way down the Malay Peninsula.

Chinese sources offer us descriptions of the emperor, clothing, aspects of daily life, and the use of ordeals as a way of deciding law cases; here, as a sample, is the unflattering Chinese description of the natives: "The men of this country are ugly and black, with curly hair. . . . The people are of a covetous nature. They have neither rites nor propriety. Boys and girls follow their penchants without restraint." [1]

However, there are various problems with these sources, which are the results of repeated copying of secondhand reports by people who did not understood well the differences between Southeast Asian societies and their own. Whatever kingdom Funan represents is likely to have been smaller and less powerful than the Chinese thought; it may well have been a loose association of coastal chiefdoms, through which Indian culture permeated. Older textbook histories usually treat Funan as a unified state or minor empire that ruled over much of Cambodia and the coasts along the Gulf of Siam from the second to the sixth centuries. However, the evidence does not really permit such a precise characterization. Settlement was largely confined to pockets here and there, and the influence of political leaders upon outlying communities was certainly variable, depending upon the fortunes of raiding parties or ritual contacts.

It is therefore difficult to sort out the actual historical relationships between Funan and its neighbors. There was a kingdom known as Champa (its people being known as Chams) in present-day southern Vietnam, and Chinese records speak for the Lin-yi people, who may have been Chams or may have been a separate group, farther north in Vietnam. The Vietnamese people themselves at first lived in the north, in the Red River area, and only gradually expanded southward.

The earliest inscriptions belonging to the area of Funan were records of deeds by rulers in the fifth and sixth centuries. These rulers had Sanskrit names and titles, and surrounded themselves with the paraphernalia of the Indian court. They sponsored Indian rituals, and they supported communities of Brahmans and Buddhist monks. The language of the earliest writings they left for us to read, Sanskrit, was the language of Indian temples and courts. The presence of all these Indian institutions certainly seems to show Indian influence. We have the corroboration of Chinese sources, which refer to the coming of communities of Indian holy men to the principalities of Southeast Asia. As the *T'ai-p'ing Yu-lan* says about Tun-sun, a small state in the area, "In this country there are ... two Buddhists, and more than a thousand Indian brahmans. The people of Tun-sun practice their doctrine and give them their daughters in marriage." The Khmer people too were well acquainted with the elements of Hindu religion. The kingdoms of Southeast Asia, we might well think, began their careers with Indian stars to guide them.

INDIAN INFLUENCE ON ANCIENT SOUTHEAST ASIA

It is not as simple as this, however. "Indianization" has been much discussed. There is an accepted repertoire of facts about apparent Indian influence, but scholars have been unable to agree on the correct way to interpret it: does it represent a sort of cultural colonization, with India planting the seeds of higher civilization in Southeast Asia, or is the Indian influence merely superficial, unimportant to the understanding of local society?

The actual mechanism of the process by which the Indian influence first came to Southeast Asia is not clear. There is no evidence for military colonization and massive Indian immigration. Traders must have played a part in the cultural interaction, and archaeology has been producing more and more evidence of early trade contacts. Indians were interested in gold, spices, and various forest products. Their settlements were not springboards for colonization, but they may well have been sources of strong cultural influence. Their demand for commodities originating inland may well have had an indirect but powerful effect upon the social organization of the communities in the interior; inland chieftains who controlled access to valuable products could have exploited their advantage and become dominant figures in more centralized political organizations that could turn into urban centers and embryos of Indian-style kingdoms.

On this hypothesis, both Indians and locals played active parts in the dynamics of the process. Indians came to Southeast Asia, some no doubt at the invitation of local rulers. Immigrants would have included the priestly architects of temples, called *sthapaka*, and others would have been skilled in Sanskrit verse composition. We can see this process at work later in the period of Angkor itself. Inscriptions named some priests, such as the scholarly brahman Divakarabhatta, who was born near Mathura and married a sister of Jayavarman v; he may be the author of some inscriptional verse in polished Sanskrit. Facts such as these are clear enough, but lacking evidence, we can only speculate how things happened when Indian culture first came.

Were the local people "Indianized," or was Indian culture localized? Recent years have seen a pronounced trend toward an emphasis on autonomy rather than Indianization. According to this view, the insistent and grandiose Indianness of Angkor—its majestic shrines to the gods of Hinduism, its towering bodhisattvas, its elegant Sanskrit poetry, its kings who adopted Indian names and described their empires as if they belonged in Indian myth—was all a veneer for essentially Khmer traditions and needs, a language that, despite its foreign origin, served to communicate Cambodian ideas.

What are we to make of all this? One part of the answer is that the current interest in understanding things in their local context is all to the good. History is all about context. The meaning of any form of cultural expression is likely to be lost on us if we fail to relate it to its users' own environment. On one level, we can see the Khmer use of Indian motifs as a language for the expression of Khmer cultural forms.

Perhaps, though, it is possible to go too far in this direction, denying the Indian character of anything we find. Maybe indeed we can interpret a statue, or a poem in Sanskrit, or a dance telling a story from the Ramayana, as a way of expressing an essentially Khmer idea; this does not mean that it is not also an essentially Indian idea, or that Khmers failed to participate in the Indian cultural world.

We need to take into account the structure and dynamics of a civilization such as India's. India is best seen as a seething cauldron of culture on the move, not a monolith with a single eternal message. Ideas, images, myths, doctrines, and all the apparatus of traditional culture flourished in particular places, were picked up and patronized in royal courts, acquired more elaborate forms, including literary representations, spread to far distant places, or alternatively, when kingdoms foundered, languished and retreated to the status of local folk memory. Great gods absorbed local myths or were absorbed into them, so that everywhere in Indian civilization there were and are countless discrepant versions of every cult, every story, every belief. The whole civilization consists of a mosaic of jostling traditions, and for a while, much of Southeast Asia became part of this mosaic.

Angkor belongs in this picture. Its rulers patronized Indian religious cults lavishly, especially that of Shiva, and its sculpture illustrated in depth the repertoire of Indian myth and epic legend. At the same time, Indian motifs were given local twists and made to express local ideas; everywhere were special forms lacking counterparts in India. Innovations were made in the iconography; Vishnu came to be accompanied by a crocodile or lizard, and the god Agni appeared mounted on a rhinoceros. Temple design evolved in ways unmatched in India. But by the same token, every locality *within* India had and has its own special local twists by which Indian themes are reinterpreted to express local traditions. What we should conclude, then, is that Cambodia's relationship with Indian civilization involved a complex process of interaction. We should avoid opposite mistakes—it is not true that India colonized in any sense; nor is it true that Indian culture in Cambodia was something exotic and alien, irrelevant to local society except by being reinterpreted in local terms.

INDIGENOUS KHMER RELIGION

In both India and Southeast Asia, religion has traditionally provided the language of cultural identity. To understand cultural history, we need to understand religion. What sort of religion existed when the Indian influences came?

No detailed records describe this religion. Archaeology offers hints, but for the most part it has to be reconstructed by assuming that it was rather like the types of folk religion found in better-known places or at later times in Cambodia. Coedes attempted a summary of the features of Southeast Asian prehistoric religion: animism, cults of ancestors, cults of the gods of the earth, shrines erected in high places, and burial of the dead.

"Animism," is a broad concept capable of describing many forms of religion in many places, where it develops spontaneously within the culture of small communities with subsistence economies. To be more precise, animism is the belief in spirits present in features of the environment, spirits that can (at least in certain circumstances) communicate with living people and affect their fortunes. They may be associated with the earth or with particular pieces of land, hills, rivers, trees, stones, or almost any other feature of the environment or aspect of human life.

Animism, on this interpretation, certainly characterizes much in the religion of Cambodia. It is based on locality; spirits have power in particular places, where they stay as long as there are people to maintain their cult, regardless of the rise and fall of kingdoms. It is therefore quite possible that, at the folk level, modern Khmer practices display the general character of a style of religion that has endured in the region since prehistoric times.

The most conspicuous type of Khmer spirit is the *neak ta*, which is normally linked to a particular community and functions as a guardian spirit. These spirits are everywhere. Offerings are made to them in shrines, typically in the form of a roughly made miniature house on stilts—a *khtom*—facing a tree, where the spirit is believed to reside. If these offerings are properly maintained, the spirit will promote the good fortune of its devotees.

An example of the subtle interaction of indigenous religion with Indian is the adaptation of the *neak ta* within the Buddhist system. Sometimes Buddhist monks would take part in rituals addressed to the *neak ta*. Sometimes local tree spirits would be designated as *sotapan*, spiritually advanced beings destined for Buddhist enlightenment, and cults addressed to them would find new Buddhist legitimacy.

Alongside the *neak ta* and not always distinguished from them are various sorts of spirit that can influence people's lives. Sometimes these are mischievous and potentially harmful, especially if they are the ghosts of people who died prematurely. Around any village are believed to exist various unseen beings who can bring good or evil, some the ghosts of humans, some identified with the forces of nature. In the forest dwell dangerous goblins, and folklore abounds in stories of the terrible punishments inflicted on the unlucky or the unwary by malicious or vengeful beings, sometimes taking on human form to trap their victims. The spirits are divided into many distinct categories. Most of the names of these categories are Khmer; others are taken from Sanskrit, such as *devata*, "divinity."

One particularly important category of spirit belonging to Khmer folk religion is the *naga*, or snake. Admittedly, the word itself is Indian; but it is interesting that within India this term was an indigenous one adopted into Sanskrit from local sources, where cults were addressed to powerful and dangerous serpent spirits dwelling in the waters and beneath the earth. In Southeast Asia, the word *naga* came into use for the spirits of just such indigenous spirits. For example, underneath the earth lurks the serpent spirit Krong Peali, who owns all the land and must be propitiated when people wish to build. In the Khmer religious imagination, *nagas* are ubiquitous and can be ignored only at one's peril; Indian snake myths, when they came to the Khmer empire, served to give iconographical and mythic form to notions that were already deeply rooted in culture.

All this represents the activity of a layer of religion that has existed since prehistoric times and has coexisted with imported religious systems, often molding them to serve its own purposes, while acquiring more elaborate cults. With the coming of Hinduism and Buddhism, the indigenous spirits continued to watch over the village communities, while the Indian deities watched over their temples, or over kingdoms, in much the same way.

THE INSCRIPTIONS

The earliest inscriptions in the region used the Sanskrit language, and in Cambodia the record begins in the fifth century. From the seventh century there were also inscriptions wholly or partly in Old Khmer, the old form of the Cambodian language, much influenced in its vocabulary by Sanskrit; the oldest dates from A.D. 612. Altogether there are about 1,200 inscriptions in Sanskrit or Old Khmer or both, covering the period to the fourteenth century.

The Angkorian period dates from about A.D. 800. We know about the previous few centuries, in which the early Khmer kingdoms developed, from a reasonably substantial body of inscriptions—virtually all records of endowments made to foundations (temples or shrines), dedicated to gods who usually had Sanskrit names. A recent count of the pre-Angkorian inscriptions puts the number at over 230, with a further 40 unpublished.

The purpose of the inscriptions was presumably to establish a permanent record attesting the munificence of the donors. The information given by the inscriptions varies from many to almost nothing, but generally follows a set pattern. If there is an opening Sanskrit section, it offers a eulogy of the god at the center of the cult, or a eulogy of the donor making the endowment and his family, or both. Often there are genealogical details of his family, sometimes including legendary ancestors. Particulars of the goods donated follow. These are brief in Sanskrit sections, but Old Khmer sections give more information, with details about the land acquired to give to temples and lists of such other items as food, utensils, and the staff and servants whose services the donor controlled and made over to the upkeep of the foundation.

PRELUDE TO ANGKOR

What do we learn of historical value from these sources? In some ways it is very limited. Earlier generations of scholars concentrated upon the construction of genealogies of kings and their dates, but although there are many claims and scraps of information about particular individuals and their families, they do not come together well; attempts to construct orderly narratives of dynasties and their kingdoms have all run into trouble. Clearly, there was much competition across the Khmer territory between various rival lords, many of them adopting Indian titles and making claims to kingship.

It is useful, though, to identify two main stages. The first corresponds to the period of "Funan," lasting from the early centuries until the sixth. The language of the inscriptions belonging to this stage has been described as representing a more southerly variant of Khmer dialect. Funan was based in the south, with large settlements near the coast in what is now Vietnam. The second stage appears to correspond to the florescence of the kingdoms known to the Chinese as Chenla, from the end of the sixth century to the end of the eighth. Earlier historians, influenced by Chinese accounts, supposed that the shift was the result of conquest of Funan by Chenla, based in the north. In fact the transition seems not to have been so dramatic; inscriptions suggest considerable political continuity, but the details are unclear. Chinese sources vouch for the continued existence of Funan in the seventh century, when it sent embassies. Inscriptions refer to various rulers in different places, but the genealogical and territorial connections between them are obscure. Some rulers were able to extend their sway over large areas. Isanavarman I appears to have ruled over most of Cambodia from 610 to circa 628. This was a major stage along the way toward Khmer unification. Jayavarman I, who reigned from about 657, appears to have consolidated a large kingdom; his capital may have been in what later became the heartland of Angkor.

The picture is clear enough in broad outline. The Khmer territory was an arena of competing communities, some subject to chieftains or lords who were able to aspire to the status of Indian-style kings. In the Funan period, the main centers were in the south, where the trade was. In the seventh and eighth centuries, however, in the Chenla period, two things happened: some of the principalities were growing bigger, gaining more abundant resources and territory; and they were gravitating to the north.

Michael Vickery has suggested possible reasons for this. The economy of the old Funan declined as trade routes now bypassed its formerly favored coast. Rulers inland sought to extend their territorial overlordship to new areas where other resources could be found. This expansion took two important possible directions. One was northeast, into the Cham territories (now weakened politically by the temporary move southward of the Cham capital district), where commercially valuable commodities including iron and other metal deposits were to be found. The other was northwest, right across into the area of Battambang, where the fertile land was good for rice agriculture. The growth of populations and of state organizations with sophisticated urban culture made both these areas important potential sources of power. Angkor, which followed on after the Chenla period, happened to be strategically placed between them. This fact may well have much to do with Angkor's success.

JAYAVARMAN II AND THE BEGINNINGS OF ANGKOR

The name *Angkor* is derived ultimately from the Sanskrit *nagara*, literally "city" but often used more widely for a royal city and the territory controlled by the monarch—that is, in effect, a kingdom or state. Angkor is now used to identify the Cambodian kingdom and empire that exercised authority fairly continuously over at least a very great part of the Khmer population from about A.D. 800 to the fifteenth century. The name is also often used to designate the urban area north of Tonle Sap Lake where most kings had their capitals, and where the remains of the monuments they built are densely concentrated.

Eventually, the rulers of Angkor looked back to Jayavarman II as the founder of their state; sometimes their inscriptions traced their own descent back to him, though the web of genealogical relationships linking the rulers is complicated and obscure. The claims of later kings to be descended from Jayavarman II cannot be regarded as evidence of actual legitimacy according to a definite and effective rule of succession. Jayavarman did not leave inscriptions telling us about himself; what we know has to be pieced together from later and sometimes unreliable sources.

Textbooks usually date the beginning of Jayavarman's reign, and hence the formal inauguration of Angkor, to A.D. 802, the year when a particular ritual of consecration took place. However, Jayavarman had by then been effectively ruling over a growing kingdom from some time before, perhaps from 790, and his reign lasted until about 835.

In some respects, this reign does not mark a decisive break with the earlier history of the Khmer region. Jayavarman's roots were in the society of Chenla, where a network of lordly families, with home bases in different parts of the Khmer territory, competed for power; Jayavarman was one of the most successful, although it is probable that neither he nor his successors really exercised genuine central control over the entire Khmer territory until very much later. His name begins no new series in the lists of Khmer rulers drawn up by modern scholars; a Jayavarman I, after all, was a ruler in the Chenla period.

Nevertheless, the second Jayavarman's construction of a large kingdom stretching from east to west of the Khmer territory was an important stage in the evolution of Khmer nationhood, and the Khmer people later looked back upon his assertion of Khmer independence from the over-lordship of "Java," an assertion embodied in his ritual in 802, as a celebration of their national identity. There is no doubt of the later symbolic importance of the date or of the ritual that marked it.

Jayavarman II built up his kingdom in the course of a series of campaigns during which he established, successively, temporary capitals in a number of different places. He seems to have come originally from the eastern side of Cambodia, and inscriptions record that he spent time in "Java." This could conceivably refer to the Javanese empire of the Sailendras, which was expanding aggressively in the period; but many historians think that "Java" was probably not the modern Java in Indonesia. It has been suggested that this may well be a name for Champa, to the east of Cambodia and plausibly regarded as a looming threat at the time. At all events, Jayavarman's movements took him from the southeast to the northeast, then westward across the territory to the north of the Tonle Sap Lake. Possibly receiving setbacks there, he retreated to a point east of the later Angkor and established his capital, Mahendraparvata, at the Phnom Kulen, where he had himself consecrated as universal lord, or *cakravartin* (literally "wheel turner"), and declared his independence from "Java." Before his reign was over, he finally established the capital at Hariharalaya, a short distance to the southeast of the later Angkor capital site and close to the shore of the lake. Here several successors continued to rule; not until the end of the ninth century did Angkor proper first become the site of a royal capital.

THE DEVARAJA

There is a widespread popular idea that the rulers of Asian empires such as Angkor were regarded by their subjects as more than ordinary mortals. According to this idea, they were actu-ally gods on earth. Considered as a ritual and cosmological statement, this proposition has something to be said for it; considered as a description of the political system and its practical workings, however, it is false. Nevertheless, one action of Jayavarman II has contributed power-fully to encourage it—his institution of the cult of the *devaraja*.

The name of the cult is Sanskrit, and it can indeed be translated as "god-king." This cult was solemnly inaugurated (at least according to the much later inscription that tells us about it) amid great ceremony in 802 as a declaration of the ruler's might, and this has encouraged the notion that Jayavarman and his successors were able to wield a total despotic authority by virtue of their claim to divinity.

We need to look a little more closely at the facts known about the *devaraja* to see why it does not really support such an interpretation. In 802 Jayavarman sealed his independence from "Java," and his imperial dominion over the Khmer people, by setting up the *devaraja* cult with a liturgy specially compiled by an eminent brahman, and he established a hereditary line of priests to officiate at the cult.

These facts at first encouraged scholars to believe that the cult was addressed to the king himself as a god; however, it is now recognized that this does not fit the evidence. The name, in its Sanskrit and Khmer versions, can just as well mean "king of the gods," and this suits the contexts better. Whatever it was, it centered on an icon—a bronze image of Shiva, in one theory—that was transported from place to place like a piece of royal regalia and adopted as a national guardian figure.

The high-flown language of inscriptions often makes the king equivalent to a god, it is true, and this equivalence is quite important on the level of cosmological symbolism—if the kingdom became an image of the heavens by ritual and architectural design, divine energy would underpin good fortune and prosperity. But on the plane of real life, Jayavarman and his successors were embroiled in constant conflict with rivals who treated them as fallible human obstacles to their own ambitions, far too much so to expect anything like worship as it is understood in the tradition of western religious culture.

Further, the *devaraja* cult, oddly enough, does not seem to have been at all important to most kings. It was much more important to the line of priests appointed to manage it, as the rationale for the grants and privileges enjoyed by the family. Indeed, it has even been suggested that the cult had no particular significance in the ninth century, when it was supposed to have been founded. Some scholars have argued that the *devaraja* was not essentially Indian at all; on this view, it was an indigenous Khmer deity adopted as a guardian spirit (with a name that happened to be translated into Sanskrit as *devaraja*).[2]

THE GROWTH OF INDIAN RELIGIOUS IDEAS

The Khmer rulers attached great importance to Indian motifs, at least in the symbolism and ritual of their court culture, which was permeated by Indian religious ideas. The view of the ordering of the universe that they represent was at bottom like that of indigenous Khmer tradition, with its concepts of personal spirits in the environment. The Indian cosmology similarly evolved in a society constituted of small groups living on the land, among which agriculture and urbanization gradually developed.

The earliest recorded teachings belong to the religion of the Vedas, which were composed by Brahman priests in a period of some centuries before and after 1,000 B.C., the Vedic period. These texts envisage earthly and divine realms; communication between the two is possible through elaborate ritual sacrifices to the gods. These sacrifices were conducted by brahmans and sponsored by community leaders, who thereby won benefits from the gods. Their wish lists consisted chiefly of strong sons and cows.

As this religion developed, the role of priests as knowledgeable ritual specialists became more important, and the elaboration of this ritual had to some extent the effect of making the gods cogs in its machinery. The Indian priests became a hereditary class, though later in Southeast Asia brahmanical status was not always hereditary, obtaining social status from their monopoly of the means of communication with the gods.

The gods in this ancient religious system belonged to the sky and air rather than to fixed localities on Earth. At an early stage, the lord of the gods was Indra, the warrior; his importance in post-Vedic times was chiefly as a metaphor for power and lordship. Other gods were those of the sky and earth, the sun, the wind, storm, dawn, and many others. Important was the god of fire, Agni, who had a dual role as a god himself and as the fire that burned the sacrificial offerings and summoned the other gods.

With the development of prosperous urban culture, priests became full-time specialists patronized by rulers, and they developed increasingly bookish and philosophical sets of teachings. The early Upanishads, books of interpretation attached to the Vedas, contain the doctrine that the individual self is no more than a manifestation of the supreme Self that constitutes the unity of all things; this idea remained important in mainstream Hindu thought thereafter, and was well understood by Southeast Asian literati. Another important brahmanical concept was dharma, the order of the universe; it acquired extended meanings of moral obligation, the duty of the individual in society, and righteousness.

The brahmans did not have the field to themselves. During the sixth and following centuries B.C., there was a reaction against their claims to authority as mediators between the profane and sacred realms. Wandering holy men, called *sramanas*, offered teachings rejecting brahmanical doctrines and the Vedas, sometimes in favor of more or less materialistic notions. Some, like Jainism and Buddhism, emphasized moral responsibility. Buddhism combined this with a denial of the existence of the self, either individual or cosmic.

One important idea that became pervasive from about the eighth century B.C. was that of karma—the moral law of cause and effect. According to this doctrine, which was accepted by many of the main religious groups (including the brahmans, the Jains, and the Buddhists), good actions cause later good experiences, while bad actions bring suffering. One form of reward or punishment can be rebirth in a good or bad condition; rebirth is a corollary of the doctrine, ensuring that in the long run there is a moral consequence for every action.

THE DIVINE ORDER

Conspicuous in Cambodia is the legacy of another aspect of Indian belief—its cosmography or sacred geography. In this scheme, the sacred and profane realms were linked by a sacred axis; rising through the very center of the world, it transcended ordinary time and space as it ascended to the heavens. The magic center on earth was marked by Mount Meru, home of the gods. Around Mount Meru, like courtiers, four smaller buttress mountains were disposed. At its top were the four guardian deities, lords of the four quarters of the world. At the summit presided the lord of the gods. The identity of this lord varied according to sect; in Hindu contexts it was commonly Shiva. Buddhism added further invisible realms above the summit, realms that became increasingly ethereal and turned into states in which the world and consciousness dissolved. Below, around Mount Meru, were the continents on which mortals lived. In one scheme, there were four, with India being the southernmost one. In another, seven concentric ring-shaped continents alternated with intervening oceans.

All this was well known to the monks and priests of Angkor, some of whom were Indians themselves. Angkor adopted this cosmography with zeal, seeking to map the celestial geography upon the realms of its kings so that each capital city should become the center of the world. Hence cities were laid out in square symmetry, with the shrine of the patron deity at the center, symbolizing Mount Meru. The shrine was usually raised upon a pyramidal platform, and the tower containing the presiding deity was at the center, with four smaller ones around to represent Meru's subordinate mountains. Angkor Wat itself embodies this scheme perfectly. It was also adopted by Buddhism; Angkor Thom, capital of Jayavarman VII, embodies it in a similar way, with the Bayon as Mount Meru.

A story about an earlier temple mountain, the Phimeanakas, tells how, according to custom, the king went there every night and cohabited with a *naga*, a serpent spirit in the form of a beautiful woman. If the tryst was missed, the kingdom would be destroyed.

The embodiment of Indian myth in the stones of Angkor was relentless and ubiquitous. The sculpture of all the monuments exploits at every turn the resources of narrative myths telling of the deeds of immortals. Wherever Indian culture spread, the two great verse epics, the Mahabharata and the Ramayana, made themselves at home, and scenes from these epics evidently resonated deeply in the Khmer imagination, as in other parts of Southeast Asia. The Mahabharata is really a library or compendium of teachings, legends, and stories; through it runs a narrative of two princely families brought into conflict by disputed claims to a kingdom. It leads to cataclysmic war, with the supporters of the five Pandava brothers aligned against those of their cousins, the Kauravas. All are killed in the mighty battle except the Pandava brothers. The tale can be read as an allegory on many levels.

Hugely popular in Southeast Asia too was the Ramayana, the tale of Prince Rama (who came to be regarded in Hinduism as one of the incarnations of the god Vishnu); unjustly expelled from his kingdom, he wanders in exile with his brother and his wife Sita; Sita is abducted by the demon lord Ravana; with the help of the monkey army, Rama defeats Ravana in a mighty battle, and his wife is restored to him.

Episodes from these stories, as well as illustrations from many scenes portrayed in brahmanical and Buddhist literature, are reproduced on the temple walls of Angkor, which thus become something like encyclopedias in stone.

HINDU DEITIES

Rama and Krishna are two of the avatars, or incarnations, of Vishnu; priestly theory identified ten, counting the Buddha as ninth and the horse avatar Kalkin yet to come as tenth. Vishnu himself was but one of many gods (although he and Shiva between them came to dominate or absorb the rest). A few, all familiar in Angkor, deserve to be mentioned.

Brahma, first, was the personification of the sacred energy evoked in the priestly sacrifices— hence the derivative noun *brahmana*, in English "brahman" or brahmin," priest of the sacrifice. As a personal god, Brahma never acquired much of a devoted cult following (though there were some Brahma temples), but he remained a powerful image of divine creation.

Vishnu appears in various forms, most dating from after the time of the Vedas and doubtless adopted from various regional folk myths. As Krishna, he is a great lover, who as a youth loved play and mischief, frolicking with milkmaids. He is also, to his worshipers, the creator and sustainer of the world through its cycles of evolution and extinction; between cycles, while the world is in dissolution, he reclines at rest on the body of the divine serpent Sesha. Statues of Vishnu show him with four arms holding respectively the conch, the mace, the discus, and the lotus.

Shiva appears to have evolved (with contributions from various bodies of myth) from a Vedic storm god. He is represented especially (and conspicuously so in Angkor) by the linga, a phallic symbol representing fertility and creative power. Sometimes he is portrayed enacting the cosmic dance of creation. He is also an ascetic with long tangled hair, engaged in meditation. Through his hair flowed the sacred waters of the Ganges, pouring down from heaven to become a river on earth.

Innumerable other gods with regional origins have been lost to memory. Priestly rationalizations have ordered and arranged them, often bringing them into family relationships with each other and generating new stories thereby. For example, the popular elephant-headed god Ganesha is a son of Shiva. (A sort of Just So story tells how he came to have his elephant head.) Divine animals are the mounts ridden by the gods—Brahma on the goose *hamsa*, Vishnu on the bird *garuda*, Shiva on the bull *nandin*.

Nor should goddesses be forgotten, though they usually figure as consorts of the gods—Lakshmi, goddess of fortune, is Vishnu's queen, and Sarasvati, goddess of learning, is Brahma's. Shiva's has several forms; of these, Uma and Parvati sometimes appear together, and the fierce slayer of the buffalo demon, Mahishasuramardini, is popular in Cambodia, perhaps through adaptation to a local spirit.

There are whole classes of divine beings drawn from Indian myth but often fortified by local associations. There are *apsaras*, heavenly dancers, who figure among the characters represented in traditional Cambodian dance, and *gandharvas*, heavenly musicians. Important also are the *nagas*, snake spirits. As we noticed before, these resonated strongly among the Khmer people with local spirits of the earth. Serpents figure prominently in Indian myths and Angkorian plastic art—the naga balustrades that line the approach to temples, rearing up their serpent hoods with multiple heads to confront the visitor; the serpent Sesha or Ananta, on whom Vishnu rests between world cycles; or the divine serpent used as a rope in the creation myth of the churning of the ocean of milk. There is also the serpent Mucilinda, who raised his hood over the meditating Buddha to protect him from the sun.

Priestly formulations produced new forms by combining old; the best known is the Trimurti, "three-bodied," a rather abstract deity made up of Brahma, Vishnu, and Shiva combined. The three represent creation, preservation, and destruction respectively, though in the eyes of their own followers each is the sole creator. Another composite god, familiar in Southeast Asian statuary, is Harihara, a composite form of Vishnu and Shiva, with some of the attributes of both. Such combinations represent the eclecticism that was a feature of Hinduism in India, and became even more pronounced in Southeast Asia.

THE SUCCESSORS OF JAYAVARMAN II

There is a huge gap in the record of Cambodian inscriptions from 791 to 877 (except for one in 803). Jayavarman II left no written record of his own, and little remains to attest to his activity. Nevertheless, it now appears likely that he built several monuments at his capital Mahendraparvata in the Kulen Hills, and he may also have been responsible for the early stages of major constructions at his last capital, at Hariharalaya.

The reign of his immediate successor left almost no record. However, the program of large-scale building projects to proclaim royal glory was certainly advanced by the next ruler, Indravarman I, who reigned from about 877 to 889. An inscription claimed, in a typically empty rhetorical flourish, that his rule "was like a crown of jasmine on the lofty heads of the kings of China, Champa and Java."[3]

Indravarman built the Preah Ko (consecrated in 879), a group of six towers dedicated to previous rulers (with Jayavarman II at the center) and their spouses, in the form of the Indian gods and goddesses whose images graced the six shrines. This inaugurated the practice of assimilating a human being to a deity by dedicating the god's image to the human being. Throughout the history of Angkor, this doubling of the human and divine realms was a striking feature of cult statuary.

Indravarman also consecrated (in 881) the Bakong, a great pyramidal monument intended to enshrine the king's remains after his death beneath the icon of a favored deity, thereby combining the ruler with the deity. Recent research suggests that Bakong came before the Preah Ko; it was perhaps begun by Jayavarman III, whose legacy was built upon by Indravarman. The construction of such pyramidal monuments, temple mountains, was to be in later reigns an obsessive concern of ambitious rulers, anxious to acquire a sort of immortality in the realms of their divine protectors. Indravarman also built a big reservoir. To some extent, the reservoir had practical value as a water supply; to a great extent also, it had religious or ritual significance. The king was like the creator gods of Indian myth, shaping an ordered world out of the primal ocean.

YASOVARMAN AND HIS SUCCESSORS

Angkor designates the site where most of the ancient capitals were located, north of Tonle Sap Lake and northwest of Hariharalaya. The first ruler to construct his capital there was Yasovarman I (889/90–c. 910), who made the move from Hariharalaya. He centered his kingdom symbolically on Mount Meru, conveniently embodied by the one conspicuous hill in the area, Phnom Bakheng. Later ritual centers, which clustered in the same vicinity, had to represent Mount Meru by the pyramidal shape of the national shrine monument itself.

The Phnom Bakheng monument, molded to the top of the hill, used 11.1 million cubic yards (8.5 m³) of sandstone and 4.5 million bricks. Like the Bakong, it was in the form of a terraced pyramid, with the shrine of the ruler's patron deity at the summit, but with smaller shrine towers studding all the terraces, 108 in all. This number has been seen as a deliberate astrological symbol—the number of constellations of the heavens, twenty-seven, multiplied by the four phases of the moon. The scholar who suggested this, Jean Filliozat, also pointed out that from any one side one can see just thirty-three towers, and this is the number of gods said to live on Mount Meru.

Yasovarman also made it a priority to have built a huge reservoir, the East Baray, eight times the size of Indravarman's reservoir. He built a roadway elevated on a causeway linking his capital to the old Hariharalaya site, and surrounded his capital city with an embankment defining a square two and a half miles (4 km) on a side. For all this achievement, the king remains a shadowy figure, described only by formula expressions of greatness. For example, it is said that he was a powerful warrior who could smash a block of copper into three pieces with his sword.

Such feats, even if authentic, could not intimidate people after Yasovarman's death, and it appears that Khmer unity, to whatever extent it had been achieved before, was now lost for a while. There was a substantial interlude, during which kings set up a capital elsewhere, at Koh Ker. No inscriptions attest the authority of the Koh Ker kings. However, another powerful ruler, Rajendravarman II (944–c. 968), possibly linked by his ancestry to the old Chenla royalty and with a base in the old city of Bhavapura, returned his capital to the Angkor site where he had to engage in extensive clearing and renovation.

Rajendravarman's reign followed a pattern typical of Angkor's more successful rulers, marked by the building of monuments and public works. He set up a pyramidal shrine dedicated to Shiva, the Pre Rup, by the East Baray, and another, the East Mebon, on an island in the middle of the reservoir. His empire appears to have extended into parts of what is now southern Vietnam, Laos, and northeast Thailand. He was in charge of a military expedition into the long-term rival to the east, Champa; his army entered the Cham city of Po Nagar in triumph and plundered a golden statue.

Rajendravarman appears to have imposed a measure of administrative centralization upon his empire. A uniform structure of local administration divided the realm into provinces. Genuine central control was still probably relative and temporary, depending on success in dealing with regional vested interests, but at least the *idea* of Khmer unity was working its way by fits and starts into the political culture of Angkor.

Ta Keo was Rajendravarman's temple mountain, an elaborate pyramid with surrounding cloisters. Banteay Srei, another important construction from the end of his reign, is a complex of tiny shrine towers about twelve miles (20 km) north of Angkor, moated and now surrounded by forest.

SURYAVARMAN I AND IMPERIAL POWER

The imperial idea was given a boost by the career of Suryavarman I (1002–1050), though he secured his position on the throne only after a period of conflict between rival claimants. Evidently from a home base in the east, he extended his power in the course of a series of struggles, eventually taking control of Angkor, the capital territory, in 1010. He then backdated his reign. In 1011 he had an oath of loyalty sworn to him by about 400 officials, in an attempt to consolidate royal authority: "This is the oath which we . . . swear, all, without exception, cutting our hands, offering our lives and our devotion gratefully, without fault, to His Majesty Sri Suryavarmadeva . . . in the presence of the sacred fire, of the holy jewel, the brahmans and the preceptors."[4]

Suryavarman was an energetic ruler, anxious to make a difference. He may have been responsible for the founding of Preah Khan of Kompong Svay, an important settlement about sixty miles (100 km) to the east; he built smaller reservoirs, bridges, and rest houses, and was probably responsible for the construction of the West Baray (5 by 1.2 miles [8 x 2 km]), a huge reservoir, similar in design to the Eastern Baray but .62 miles (1 km) longer.

Monument building was not neglected; Suryavarman constructed four major temples to Shiva. These centered upon linga shrines. The king's territory came to incorporate all that had belonged to his predecessors, with the probable addition of the Lopburi area in present-day Thailand, on the middle reaches of the Chao Phraya River. Part of northeastern Thailand, around Phimai, had a significant Khmer population and was incorporated within the Angkorian territory; at that time Mahayana Buddhism flourished there.

Suryavarman's reign left many inscriptions, which show the increasing use of land grants as new areas were opened up, principally to the north. Both the king and the propertied families with court positions made it a practice to bestow land, buildings, and workers upon religious foundations. Territories could be assigned to religious foundations, and particular zones within them marked out for the creation of temples and the provision of personnel. Temples thus became centers of settlement, providing a focus for population expanding into new territories.

This process is illustrated in some detail by a long inscription belonging to the reign of Suryavarman's son and successor, Udayadityavarman II (1050–c.1066). Udayadityavarman gave active patronage to the head of the family of priests attached to the devaraja cult, described above. He also deserves to be mentioned as the creator of the Baphuon, a great temple mountain whose central tower shrine was originally covered in bronze.

THE BASES OF ANGKOR'S POWER

Many kings had to fight their way to power from home bases in regional centers, and these regional centers—for example, Rajendravarman's in Bhavapura—exercised a constant centrifugal pull upon Angkor's cohesion. Multiple marriages created a web of power, bringing together the interests of the great families, but half-brothers in palaces notoriously engage in lethal competition;

the web was loose and could easily be torn or reconstituted in different ways. Many people close to the throne meant many cooks in the kitchen. The thirteenth-century Chinese visitor Chou Ta-kuan (Zhou Daguan) reported that most high officials were princes. As Claude Jacques has reminded us, only a minority of the recorded rulers of Angkor were sons or brothers of their predecessors. Most of the others, though not all, could claim some sort of family connection with predecessors, especially Jayavarman II, but they did not all come from a single clearly defined dynasty. Their real power often lay in the regions, where particular families inherited traditional authority.

On the other hand, Angkor was not just another loosely articulated regional kingdom like those of the Chenla era. A territory with a persisting economic edge over its neighbors can, other things being equal, maintain a bigger and better army longer and more effectively than its neighbors, and can turn this advantage into the construction of a relatively centralized imperial regime. There had to be an economic basis of power. Angkor was well positioned in relation to land routes and to the Mekong (with its extension to Tonle Sap Lake facilitating transport to Angkor's nearest shores), and once its rulers had colonized the area to the west, in the Battambang plain, they controlled an area suitable for rice agriculture. At its height, Angkor may have been able to extract from its agricultural workforce, in taxation, a larger surplus than neighboring states could achieve.

It is of course debatable what part, if any, was played in Angkor's agriculture by the great reservoirs, the *barays*. The debate is far from being resolved; important questions remain about the rulers' purposes in building these. If the reservoirs performed chiefly ritual functions, we need to look elsewhere for the basis of an agricultural surplus, and the direction to look, on one view, is westward—to the Battambang plain, with its fertile rice lands. It was perhaps the extension of territorial control to this area that enabled Angkor's rulers to keep their coffers replenished. (See Goodman essay, p. 256.)

Power comes from the blade of a sword. Angkor controlled considerable military power. We do not have reliable statistics, but we know that armies could be large; indeed, a Chinese account claimed that Angkor could field 200,000 elephants and many horses, but figures like this are all too likely to be fanciful. In the thirteenth century Chou Ta-kuan reported that in a recent war there had been universal conscription of adult males; this is likely to represent a dire emergency situation.

We can read in the inscriptions the insignia of a military culture where martial values prevailed. Soldiers used sabers, as well as broadswords, daggers, catapults, and ballistae carried on elephants or on wheeled trolleys. Elephants were a major feature (if arguably a counterproductive one) of Indian warfare. Angkor also had a navy; in one campaign Angkor was able to send 700 ships of its own around the coast to Vietnam.

This was an imperial state, with a court culture pervaded by the values of imperial grandeur. We cannot tell what the ordinary subjects thought about it all. Some historians nowadays think that the farming population must have resented the burden, in tax and conscripted labor, imposed by the court to support the public works and military campaigns. Others think that the population participated willingly, recognizing the material and religious benefits. Nobody really knows. Perhaps, for most people, the king was a remote figure, so remote as to seem almost supernatural; and people like to blame their ills upon known familiar villains close at hand such as landlords and tax collectors. Villagers in this situation might see themselves as victims of injustices, which however the king would remove if he knew about them.

SURYAVARMAN II AND ANGKOR WAT

Kings of Angkor took names implying that they sought refuge in divine forces. *Surya* is a name for the sun, formerly a powerful deity in parts of India. A second sun king came to power in the following century: Suryavarman II (1113–c. 1150).

This king had quite close family connections with the two kings before him, Jayavarman VI and Dharanindravarman I, but he had to fight his way to power, like so many other rulers. His reign was marked by wars, especially against the old enemies the Chams. The relationship between Angkor and Champa was one of more or less permanent enmity, with the advantage seesawing up and down; Suryavarman invaded Cham territory successfully and put his brother-in-law on the throne in the Cham capital, Vijayapura.

Suryavarman also had relationships with China. According to a Chinese source, Angkor at this time extended northward as far as Champa, eastward as far as the sea, westward as far as Pagan (the powerful Buddhist-influenced Burmese empire that superseded earlier smaller kingdoms), and southward down the peninsula to Grahi.

The empire appears to have been at the height of its power. The creation of Angkor Wat was the crowning achievement of Suryavarman's reign, but it should not be allowed to overshadow his other activities.[5] Like other ambitious rulers, Suryavarman sought to mark his reign by the construction of a Mount Meru right at the center of his dominions, an impressive shrine built at the heart of the capital site. His shrine was Angkor Wat.

Angkor Wat has long held a fascination for the Khmer people and visitors alike, and myths have grown up around it. One local legend, for example, tells of its founding by a half-divine being who was taken up to heaven but eventually forced to leave; as a compensation he was given the design of a heavenly mansion to build as his temple mountain at the center of his kingdom on earth.

The extraordinary reputation of this monument may be unfair to the other magnificent creations of Angkor's builders, but Angkor Wat is a superb creation. The name *Wat* is strictly inappropriate, as it is the modern name for a Buddhist establishment; since the passing of Angkor, Cambodia has been committed to Theravada Buddhism, and communities of saffron-robed Theravada monks are nowadays to be seen among the ancient monuments. But Angkor Wat was dedicated primarily to Vishnu, the Hindu god, who incidentally is sometimes linked to sun cults.

It has survived the passage of time better than most monuments, partly because the moat around its large precinct has slowed down the encroachment of the forest. Around the central tower are four subordinate shrines (Meru's buttress mountains). The five towers rise above three terraces surrounded by cloisters where galleries contain the famous relief carvings. The surrounding complex of courtyards, cloisters, and free-standing buildings was bounded by a sandstone and laterite wall defining a rectangle .93 by .80 miles (1.5 by 1.3 km). This was large enough to contain not only the royal palace but also the government's administrative center, virtually a city in its own right.

From this city, Suryavarman commanded an empire that must have seemed (once the rival Cham kingdom was dealt with) possessed of an impregnable glory.

INSTABILITY AT THE CENTER

If there was stability, it did not last. After Suryavarman's death, the throne was occupied by successive claimants in quick succession. Technically, according to inscriptions, his successor was Dharanindravarman II, but this claimant seems never to have held power at Angkor. Yasovarman II came next, only to come to a violent end at the hands of an impatient usurper, Tribhuvanaditya, who himself was later to be the victim of the conquest of Angkor by Champa. Angkor's political history graphically illustrates the old maxim, Uneasy lies the head that wears the crown.

The Cham invasion, in 1177, was a major reverse. The Khmer people were frequently in conflict with their neighbors, but they were unaccustomed to humiliating defeat. According to one story, a Chinese mandarin shipwrecked in Champa taught the Cham cavalry to use bows and arbalests and to fire while riding; if so, this could have given the Chams a decisive advantage. They came upon Angkor in a surprise move that brought them in ships across the Great Lake. For a while, they were able to put their own king, Jaya Indravarman IV, on the Khmer throne. Their occupation was destined to be brief, however. It provided the stimulus for a Khmer prince, hitherto aloof from the succession disputes, to mount a vigorous challenge to the Cham occupation. That prince, taking the throne as Jayavarman VII, was to inaugurate in Angkor one last age of imperial glory.

BUDDHISM

Jayavarman VII, more than any other monarch, supported Buddhism, exploiting Buddhist images and concepts freely to provide a cosmological foundation for his authority. This is therefore an appropriate point at which to look more closely at the Buddhist alternative as a stream in Khmer religious culture. In Southeast Asia as a whole, Buddhism had from the beginning been a major force. Later, in the closing chapters of Angkor's history, the Theravada form of it was to spread among the Khmer people. In modern times, Theravada has become the mainstream religious tradition in Myanmar, Thailand, Cambodia, and Laos.

We need to step back to the Indian genesis of the Buddhist tradition, for its Cambodian followers were perfectly capable of studying its Indian forms with subtlety and insight. Sometimes they studied under traveling Buddhist scholars; sometimes they made pilgrimages to sacred Buddhist sites in India.

The Buddha lived in about the fifth century B.C. (the date has recently been subject to debate) in northeastern India and Nepal. Unlike some of the other wandering teachers, he accepted the idea of karma and rebirth, interpreting it in a moral sense: what brings about a good or bad result for the performer of a deed is the intention behind it.

According to Buddhism, the Hindu gods are real, but they are not special—they are all just beings like ourselves working through the results of old karma and creating new, on the way from one life to another. The best sort of rebirth is not as a god but as a human, as that is the most suitable springboard for gaining enlightenment. The Buddha emphasized the impossibility of lasting peace or satisfaction in worldly life, where everything is impermanent and insubstantial. The highest goal is not just good rebirth, it is salvation—canceling out all karma by advanced spiritual cultivation, leading to enlightenment. An enlightened being, like the Buddha or some of his disciples, would not be reborn even in a heaven, but would enter nirvana.[6]

Buddhism was important in the early stages of Southeast Asian history. Inscriptions and archaeological finds attest the activity of Buddhist monks who traveled far and wide, and Buddhist images were imported or made in the area. Monks often traveled with groups of merchants, and a popular Buddhist image was Buddha Dipankara, a form of the Buddha who is represented as calmer of the waters, apt as a patron for sea voyagers. From certain periods, many seals have survived that are inscribed with a formula of Buddhist belief. Many rulers gave support to Buddhism, especially in the area of Myanmar and Thailand where Mon and Pyu kingdoms flourished.

Buddhism cannot be treated as an undifferentiated single system of practice and belief. Its historical evolution was complex, but there came to be two main divisions. The first is constituted by the old schools, which emphasized traditions and scripture. One of these old schools survives today in strength, the Theravada school, literally "wisdom of the elders."7 However, Theravada's main early influence was in Myanmar and the Mon country; only from the thirteenth century, in the closing stages of Angkor's history, did it gain a wide following in the Cambodian area, and its rise is first marked in the inscriptional record by the use of Pali in 1309.

However, the second broad division of Buddhist life, the Mahayana, was much more influential in Cambodia during the period of Angkor and inspired the most conspicuous images employed by Jayavarman VII. Developing around the beginning of the Christian era, it began as a new trend or emphasis among monks in the old schools, but as it became stronger and spread geographically, it became increasingly separate.

The difference in ideas between the two divisions is historically important, even though both share basic scriptures and doctrines. Theravada emphasizes the humanity of the Buddha as a human being who left the earth when he died, not to be reborn.

Mahayana, on the other hand, focuses on one implication of the rebirth doctrine: already, now, there are many future Buddhas (called bodhisattvas) going through lives of great spiritual achievement. Some dwell in the heavens, accessible to human supplication. Further, in an important development, new Mahayana scriptures redefined the Buddha as an eternal creative principle underlying the universe, manifested in different worlds and in different forms. Mahayana interpreted karma as something that could be transferred; this meant that, for example, a bodhisattva, who had accumulated a great store of good karma, could bestow some upon devotees and thereby answer their prayers. Everything depended on the true spiritual state of the devotees, but it was possible to incorporate in Buddhism by these means features of devotional religion.

Buddhism was a permanent subordinate stream in the religious life of Angkor; Buddhist temples were sometimes given significant endowments by rulers. However, the most characteristic form of a Buddhist monument—the stupa form—is generally lacking in Angkor's architectural repertoire. A stupa is a solid structure, conspicuous for the spire above its dome, built as a memorial to the Buddha; early stupas housed his bodily relics. Angkor's Buddhist monuments, though, consist of chambered towers housing images, like the Hindu temples.

In the earlier centuries, Buddhist scholar monks traveled back and forth along the trade routes of Southeast Asia, often taking this route at the beginning or end of sojourns in China. In the Funan and Chenla periods, a few inscriptions attest to Buddhist activities. Jayavarman VII most spectacularly gave his support to Mahayana Buddhism, to some extent grounding the legitimacy of his rule in Buddhist mythology.

JAYAVARMAN VII

The prince who later, as king, took the reign name Jayavarman, the seventh in the Khmer series, was far away in Champa, involved in a military campaign, when Yasovarman II (c. 1150–c. 1165) lost his throne to the usurper Tribhuvanaditya. Anxious to restore legitimacy, an inscription tells us, Jayavarman hurried back, but then had to bide his time, "waiting for the propitious moment to save the land heavy with crimes."

That moment came when the Chams had staged their successful invasion in 1177, striking a devastating blow at the Angkor heartland after an unexpected approach across Tonle Sap Lake. This prompted Jayavarman to act. Casting himself as a liberator, he succeeded in ousting the invaders in a matter of months; his later foundation of the Preah Khan temple at Angkor marked the site of his victory. But further campaigning was necessary; not until 1181 could he claim to have mastered the country. It seems that he could not easily rely upon anything like a nationalistic sentiment to sweep him to power. Perhaps the old institutions of royal pomp and circumstance, with their Hindu topdressing, were losing their grip on people's loyalty, and the legitimacy of the old regime was wearing thin. However that may be, Jayavarman gave pronounced favor to Buddhism, a new ideology for a new regime.

He was eventually able to assert power over the Khmer territories ruled by his predecessors; an inscription of 1191 asserts that his washing water was supplied by the rulers of Java and the "two kings of the Chams," among others. A relief carving at Banteay Chhmar portrays the king undergoing a ritual of consecration at a site that could be at Rong Chen in the Kulen Hills, where the founding monarch Jayavarman II proclaimed independent dominion. If so, it was a highly symbolic reenactment.

Jayavarman proceeded to assert his power in a series of grand gestures, most especially by his building program, which gave Angkor as many monuments again as it already possessed. It is now recognized that he is unlikely to have seen the completion of all the construction projects for which he was responsible; much of the credit should probably be given to his successor, about whom not much is otherwise known, for the continuation of the building program. Jayavarman's achievement as the guiding spirit behind a significant proportion of the art and architecture illustrated in this volume is nevertheless prodigious. Here, though, there is space only for a few bare facts.

The Khmer people did not bow down to their kings as gods, but Jayavarman certainly considered himself to have a divine mission. Perhaps he saw himself as a bodhisattva—a future Buddha, capable of bestowing good fortune upon his subjects and alleviating their sufferings by the radiation of his merit. His attachment to Buddhism was explicit: an inscription tells us that he learned it from his father, who "found his satisfaction in this nectar that is the religion of Sakyamuni."[8] *Sakyamuni* is a title of the Buddha, "seer of the Sakya clan."

Jayavarman has left us real portrait statues. The practice of combining human dignitaries with patron gods is well attested in Angkorian statuary; what is unusual is that some statues appear to represent not primarily the iconography of the god but the physical likeness of the donor, Jayavarman. It has been suggested that these represent him as a worshiper, receiving the announcement that he was destined to become a Buddha; this in Mahayana Buddhism marks the beginning of a bodhisattva's career.

Like a bodhisattva, the ruler presented himself as an angel of compassion. As an inscription declares, "The physical afflictions of the people caused him mental affliction, which is all the more hard to bear; for kings are made to suffer by the people's suffering, not by their own" (Ta Prohm inscription). Jayavarman's role as a benign father figure led him to establish 102 institutions for the benefit of the sick. These are often described as hospitals, but they may have been storehouses for medicines, to which the ruler contributed from the resources of his treasury a token array of herbs.

Another practical measure was the construction of a network of major roads, built on embankments up to sixteen or twenty feet (5 or 6 m) high and running from the capital to the extremities of the Khmer country, for example a road 140 miles (225 km) long to Phimai, now in northeastern Thailand. These were punctuated by establishments called Houses of the Sacred Flame, 121 in number; their purpose, probably involving ritual, is unclear.

Jayavarman also constructed a reservoir, the Jayatataka, to the north of the East Baray, though much smaller. This fit into a pattern: successive rulers moved their public works farther upstream, perhaps superseding older constructions downstream that were degenerating. In the middle of the Jayatataka stands the Neak Pean, a complex of tanks and smaller shrines surrounding a central tank and a central shrine placed on a naga over a lotus. Though originally Hindu, it represents themes in Buddhist mythology, and the symbolism of the whole complex appears to assimilate the reservoir to Lake Anavatapta, the mythical source of the four sacred rivers of India.

Some of the ruler's projects were huge religious establishments that must have been magnets of wealth and population, becoming centers of economic life. Two big foundations outside the city walls at Angkor, both Buddhist, were at the Ta Prohm and the Preah Khan sites, both sheltering great teams of holy men, attendants, and servants, and commanding an enormous labor force. The Ta Prohm foundation, dedicated in 1186 and called Rajavihara, covered 150 acres (60 hectares) and employed 12,640 people; 79,365 people were attached to its service in agricultural areas. The Preah Khan, dedicated in 1191, employed over a thousand religious teachers, and 97,840 laborers worked to provide supplies, including about eleven tons of rice a day. Another temple organized on the same lines was the Preah Khan of Kompong Svay. This was an earlier foundation; Jayavarman refurbished it and provided it with an array of divinities focusing especially on the bodhisattva Avalokitesvara but incorporating brahmanical gods as well. Jayavarman's temples are notable for the sheer quantity of icons they housed—over 500 major gods at the Preah Khan of Angkor, and about 400 at the Ta Prohm. Brahmanical and indigenous deities figure in the lists, but Buddhism is central. In some of the main foundations we find a specific pattern; Buddhism is represented by images in the central shrine as well as to the east and south, the most auspicious directions, while Vishnu appears to the west and Shiva to the north.

Temples like these were virtually colonies, playing a part in the redistribution of economic wealth. Donations to temples were a way of earning religious merit, and it is not surprising that some of them became rich. Their treasures represent a great piling up of resources. For example, the listed property of one foundation included 35 diamonds, 40,620 fine pearls, 4,540 precious stones, 967 *voiles de chine*, and 512 silk beds. Temple endowment at all times played a complex role in society: not only could it earn religious merit, enhancing prestige, but there were also tax advantages in making over property to temples, and a donor family could win priestly careers there for its members.

Jayavarman's new capital was Angkor Thom, north of Angkor Wat and tucked between the East and West Barays. The new national shrine representing Mount Meru, the center of the city physically and of the world symbolically, was the Bayon, a huge stone pile dedicated to the patron bodhisattva Avalokitesvara in the form of Lokesvara. The Bayon maintains the architectural motifs of earlier temple-mountains, with a pyramid of terraces and towers, but its design is complex and tangled, representing several successive plans. The shrine towers jostle densely, occupying a polygon instead of the previously favored neat square.

The Bayon is famous for its galleries of relief sculptures, which betray a preoccupation with the real world in which the artists lived. Detailed scenes depict real armies, not fantasy ones from Indian epics. We see troops on the march followed by a train of oxcarts with woven covers and precariously packed bundles on the backs of elephants. Lines of bowmen aim upward, judging the right trajectory. There are also views of townsfolk at work and play—engaged in a cockfight, in a game of chess with big bulky chessmen, and haggling at the market, where there are jeweled women in *sampots* and fiercely gesturing men. These are valuable historical documents, displaying the real life of Angkor in a way that almost nothing else can do. The inner gallery of the Bayon, it should be added, also displays certain relief panels likely to have been added in a later reign.

Most conspicuous of all the new features of the Bayon's design is the striking motif of the four faces. The upper levels of every shrine tower are sculpted into huge faces that gaze solemnly out into space—north, south, east and west. On one level, these may represent the benign omnipresence of the ruler himself, but the religious reference is another matter. There are perhaps deliberate resonances of the four-faced Hindu god of creation Brahma, but it is generally recognized that the faces are those of Avalokitesvara Samantamukha, the bodhisattva who looks down upon the world in compassion. (See Sanday essay, p. 170).

Jayavarman's reign marked a peak of royal pomp and glory, exploiting to the full the potential of Indian court culture for grandeur. Inscriptions tell of great deeds, and stones prove that some of them were real. But it was not to last; surprisingly quickly, after Jayavarman, the output of inscriptions and stone monuments dropped away, and some at least of the pomp and glory faded, although for a long time kings continued to surround themselves with lavish ceremonial and conspicuous signs of power, and Angkor was still regarded as a rich country.

At all events, the reign of Jayavarman VII came to an end sometime before 1120 and after 1214. Perhaps he thought that, after his death, things would continue as before, but destiny was to prove otherwise.

THE LAST STAGES

The next king was Indravarman II, who reigned until 1243. As noted above, he may have contributed to the completion of some of the monuments undertaken by his predecessor. There is a floating legend about a "leper king" of Angkor, which could conceivably be attached to him, but we can only speculate.

Much of what can be said of the next ruler, Jayavarman VIII, is also speculation. To a great extent the Buddhist sculpture and statuary of his reign has been deliberately defaced at a later time; attempts have been made to erase the distinctively Buddhist features and replace them with Hinduism. Jayavarman VIII may have been the ruler responsible for this "Hindu backlash," as it has been called. At any rate, Mahayana Buddhism was not to regain favor. Theravada was gaining ground, as Chou Ta-kuan, the Chinese visitor at the end of the thirteenth century, mentions. One monument, the Preah Palilay, shows Theravada influence; it is the only essentially Buddhist monument in Angkor untouched by the iconoclasm of Hindu zealots, perhaps because it postdated the anti-Buddhist movement.

Chou Ta-kuan, who was in Cambodia in 1296–97, left a detailed account of his visit, an important historical document that gives eyewitness accounts of events, places, and people. Chou offers a window on everyday life with his comments on royal processions and the groups of people involved in them, the marketplace and the goods traded, the resident community of Chinese merchants, the color of people's skin, the workings of justice, the sanitation and hygiene of the capital, sexual habits, slavery, and much more. He provides evidence for the gradual spread of Theravada Buddhism at the time, mentioning the characteristically saffron-robed monks who subsequently became such a familiar sight in mainland Southeast Asia.

Here is part of his account of royal audiences, in which both government business and private citizens' problems were dealt with:

"Twice each day the king holds audience for the affairs of government. There are no fixed agenda. Those officials or commoners who wish to see the sovereign sit on the ground to wait for him. . . . Two girls of the palace raise the curtain with their tiny fingers, and the king, holding the sword in his hand, appears at the golden window. Ministers and common people clasp their hands and strike the ground in front of them; when the sound of the conches stops, they can raise their heads again. . . . When business is concluded, the prince returns; the two girls let the curtain fall, and everyone rises."[9]

Chou also refers to a recent war against the Thais. The rise of the Thai kingdom of Sukhothai earlier in the century was the thin end of a long wedge; during the following two centuries Cambodia became more and more threatened as Thai power in the region was consolidated. In the fourteenth century, the establishment of the Thai kingdom of Ayutthaya signified a further advance, and Thai forces compelled the Cambodian court to retreat temporarily from Angkor. In the endemic conflict between the Thai and Cambodian states, Cambodia ultimately got the worst of it.

Historical evidence is extremely scarce after Chou Ta-kuan, as inscriptions fell off in the following period. Only few references appear in Chinese accounts, but our chief source before the arrival of Europeans is the chronicles written at the courts of later dynasties, in Middle Khmer. These are contaminated by confused or legendary material, however, and give little solid information. After the thirteenth century Angkor, considered as a court culture that cultivated Sanskrit learning and patronized Hindu and Mahayana Buddhist temples, virtually disappears from historical view. In the earlier part of the fifteenth century a new capital in the area of Phnom Penh arose, and its court culture was dominated by primarily Theravada traditions. There was no grand stone temple building, and Pali was the language of religion.

It would be wrong, though, to treat this as a total break. A tradition faded, but the Khmer kingdom did not disappear. That the monuments came eventually to be largely overrun by the forest has contributed to the false impression that a whole civilization was lost and forgotten. The capital moved south, in fact, but the royal government continued. It certainly came off worst in conflict with Thailand eventually, but this did not mean the disappearance of a nation. Within the region's mosaic of people with a variety of cultures, a number of great families with mixed ancestry and pretensions to royal status competed for each other's thrones, and these same people generally continued to inhabit any given area regardless of the fortunes of war.

Further, Angkor as a site was not forthwith lost and forgotten. It remained as a provincial outpost; for a period in the sixteenth century, during which early Portuguese and Spanish visitors discovered Angkor, rulers reoccupied the site. Between 1546 and 1564 a king added bas-relief sculptures to the still-undecorated galleries of Angkor Wat—on the east side of the north gallery and the north side of the east gallery. Shortly before 1577, Tribhuvanadityavarman claimed to have restored Angkor Wat from the bottom up, reconstructing nine towers and sheathing them in gold. A number of further inscriptions from that period attest to the activity of pious magnates in the area, often recording their emancipation of slaves. After that, though, the curtain descends again.

CONCLUSION

The question, What brought about the end of Angkor's glory days? cannot be answered precisely. We can only speculate. Some historians have blamed Jayavarman's extravagance for the seeming abandonment of Sanskrit culture and monument building, but the connections are not clear. Stone, to be sure, may have been increasingly difficult to find and quarry. Theravada Buddhism, with its focus on ordinary individuals rather than great men, may have begun to gnaw away at the bases of the traditional Angkorian style, with its ostentation and its expense. But none of these explanations is definitive.

Jayavarman's extravagance is not a strong candidate; the spread of Theravada Buddhism and the wars against Thai forces, on the other hand, are likely factors, though not necessarily main causes. It is possible, as Michael Vickery has argued, that the causes of change lay in forces that operated beneath the surface, underlain by shifting patterns of economic activity. In the fourteenth and early fifteenth centuries, there were many diplomatic contacts between Cambodia and the Chinese imperial court; such contacts usually went with commercial activity, and trade in the area was quickening. The early decades of the Ming dynasty in China (beginning in 1368) witnessed a flurry of Chinese activity in Southeast Asian waters. If trade was important, the inland agrarian centers of population were giving way to flourishing commercial centers near the coasts. The shift from Angkor to Phnom Penh makes sense as part of this pattern.

But we do not know enough to pronounce confidently upon such questions. The significance of the issue here is as a reminder that there is much more to an understanding of Angkor's history than the doings of kings. In these pages, it has been necessary to take a rather top-down approach, concentrating on court culture and the activities of great men rather than on the life of ordinary people toiling in the fields. To some extent this is unavoidable; it is difficult to know much about the life of the ordinary people.

Historians are thus divided over fundamental economic questions. Similarly, we have no clear picture of the extent of slavery throughout the centuries of Angkor's existence. From the late ninth to the mid-tenth centuries especially, records of endowments include long lists of workers whose services were part of the donations made by benefactors; in the Sanskrit parts of the inscriptions they are referred to as *dasa,* "slave," but some scholars have refused to believe that they were really slaves in the usual sense.

Again, a clear picture of Angkor's trading relationships with other Asian powers has yet to be built up. We know about the kingdom's flourishing markets, where everything under the sun was traded: cardamom, pepper, ginger peel, beeswax, kingfisher feathers, *dammar* resin, vegetable oils, gamboge, aloes wood, precious stones, pearls, cotton cloth, silk, ceramics, rice, silver, gold, cattle, elephants, horses, pigs, even slaves, as well as incense, benzoin, lacquerware, and other craft products. However, it is still a matter for speculation what part was played by trade in shaping the country's history; perhaps the pattern of demand that rose and fell with the changing directions of trade routes had a decisive influence upon the fortunes of Angkor as a strategic center. The forces that shaped the ends of the Khmers do not reveal their actions on the surface record. The spotlight of history shows us the strutting and fretting of great men anxious for immortality, but so much of the stage on which they posture remains shrouded in darkness.

However, the potential for future advance in our knowledge of Angkor is good. For example, a research team from Sydney University in association with the EFEO, using recently processed radar imagery from the space shuttle *Endeavor* and from more recent flights under NASA's direction, is undertaking a study of Angkor. This research promises to cast a flood of light upon the economy and geography of Angkor as a massive urban complex, and at the same time to deepen our understanding of the dynamics of urbanization. It is becoming increasingly obvious that however obscure the details may be, the history of Angkor challenges us to explore one of the most vital cultures of Asia, a culture full of movement and innovation, economically, artistically, and politically.

Notes

1. See Paul Pelliot, "Le Fou-nan," *Bulletin de l'Ecole Française d'Extrême-Orient* [vol.2] (1902): 261 ff.

2. Recently an interesting article by Hiram Woodward, though, takes issue with this trend in interpretation. He denies that the Khmer forms of the cult object imply a local territorial divinity, and suggests that the central icon could have been a receptacle for the Holy Fire, an old brahmanical Indian institution. See Hiram W. Woodward Jr, "Practice and Belief in Ancient Cambodia," *Journal of Southeast Asian Studies* 32, no. 2 (2001): 249–61.

3. See Georges Coedès, *Inscriptions du Cambodge*, (Hanoi: Imprimerie d' Extrême-Orient, 1937), 1:43.

4. See Georges Coedès, "Le serment des fonctionaires de Suryavarman I," *Bulletin de l'Ecole Française d'Extrême-Orient* (1913), 13: 11–17, for the oath of the officials of Suryavarman I.

5. One important complex where he is likely to have initiated construction is at Beng Mealea, about twenty-five miles (40 km) east of Angkor in the direction of Preah Khan at Kompong Svay. It was later to be refurbished and extended as a Buddhist monument by Jayavarman VII.

6. Thus, theoretically, nirvana is the highest state. Nirvana has become an English word, but its original meaning is not easily grasped. It is not the same as the Hindu notions of union with an absolute or supreme self, but rather the disappearance of all the (actually illusory and deceptive) attributes of separate existence, a dissolution into ultimate calmness. In practice, this concept is too abstract for most ordinary Buddhists. The Buddha taught the Middle Way—on the one hand, avoiding the extremes of self-mortification practiced by some ascetics, who fasted and undertook severe austerities, while on the other also rejecting the self-indulgence of life in the world. Both extremes impede the quest for enlightenment, which must be pursued by assuming the life of a wandering mendicant holy man engaging in meditation. However, over the centuries Buddhist monks took to living in monasteries and settled down as part of the local community, where they could be teachers and advisers in return for sustenance.

7. Theravada emphasizes the values found in the old scriptures and the importance of individual spiritual effort. It has come to prevail in Sri Lanka, Myanmar, Thailand, Cambodia, and Laos. Its scriptures are in Pali, a literary language fairly similar to Sanskrit; as a sacred language, Pali has been influential in Cambodia.

8. See Georges Coedès, *The Indianized States of Southeast Asia,* trans. S. Cowing, (Australian National University Press, 1937), 173.

9. See Chou Ta-kuan, *Memoires sur les coutumes du Cambodge,* trans. P. Pelliot (1951; reprint, Paris: Siam Society, 2001), 34 ff.

THE

CENTRAL

ANGKOR

AREA

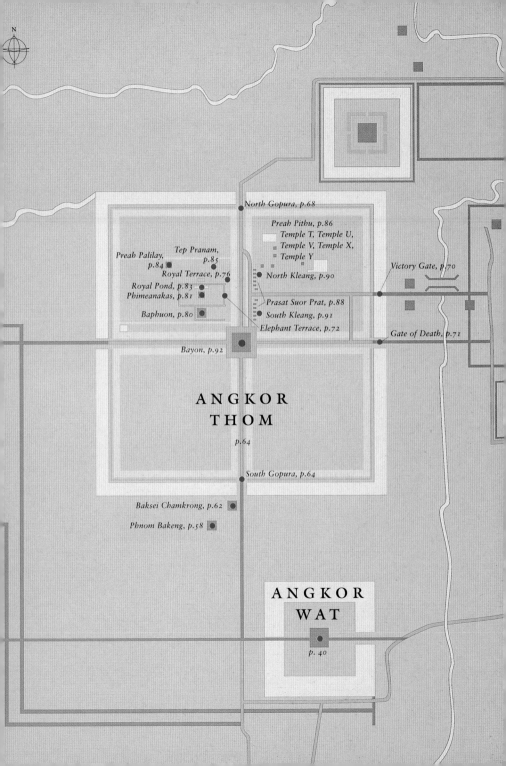

N

North Gopura, p.68

Preah Pithu, p.86
Temple T, Temple U,
Temple V, Temple X,
Temple Y

Preah Palilay,
p.84

Tep Pranam,
p.85

Victory Gate, p.70

Royal Terrace, p.76

North Kleang, p.90

Royal Pond, p.83

Phimeanakas, p.81

Prasat Suor Prat, p.88

Baphuon, p.80

South Kleang, p.91

Elephant Terrace, p.72

Gate of Death, p.71

Bayon, p.92

ANGKOR
THOM

p.64

South Gopura, p.64

Baksei Chamkrong, p.62

Phnom Bakeng, p.58

ANGKOR
WAT

p. 40

ANGKOR WAT

Angkor Wat is the
most important monument of the Khmer
civilization and the largest temple
in the world. Built by Suryavarman II,
who unified Cambodia more than
a thousand years ago,
it is widely regarded as one of the most
magnificent buildings ever created.
It was constructed as a shrine
to Vishnu, a royal mausoleum, and
a physical representation of
the Hindu cosmos.

A causeway paved with huge sandstone blocks worn smooth
by the feet of countless pilgrims crosses from the west over a wide moat.
A gopura leads to a second raised causeway, bordered by
naga balustrades intersecting with a cruciform platform called
the Grand Terrace.

A low enclosure wall, beginning near the Grand Terrace,
divided the temple from the city.
Two concentric galleries define the first and second enclosures,
with the pyramid platform at the center.

(Top) The eastern side of Angkor Wat is a secondary entrance.
The causeway crosses the moat, passes through a gopura and then a forest that still shows
faint outlines of ancient habitations, ending at the giant naga balustrades
of the third enclosure wall.

(Above) The galleries of bas-reliefs are among the largest friezes in the world,
two thousand feet (610 m) long and six and a half feet (2 m) high.
They are divided into eight major subjects, two on each side, with individual scenes in
the southwest and northwest corner pavilions.

The central sanctuary tower is the summit of the pyramid, an earthly representation of mythical Mount Meru, symbolizing the center of the world and the axis of the universe.

(Top) The idea of a curved tower, which originated in the temples of southern India, was brilliantly employed by the Khmer, who reduced the diameter and height of each successive tier, added an upturned lip of stone to fill in the shape, and redented the square corners of the structure by cutting the angles.

(Above) The exact positioning and measurements of the central sanctuary indicate that advanced astronomy played a key role in the temple's architectural design and ritual use. Extremely steep staircases, which narrow as they ascend, lead to the celestial realm of the gods.

(Opposite) Vishnu was originally installed at the apex of the central sanctuary. As the source and creator of all existence, he ruled supreme over the gods and the universe. By identifying himself with the deity, the king shared in Vishnu's glory and all-encompassing power.

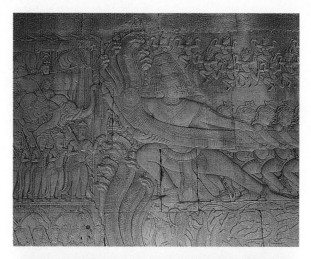

*(Top) The most famous bas-relief at Angkor
concerns the Hindu creation myth of the Churning of the Sea of Milk.
The asuras and the devas pull on either end of a great naga
wrapped around Mount Meru, which acts as a pivot, churning out
the essence of life and the universe.*

*(Above) The west gallery displays scenes from
the Hindu epic the Ramayana, in which monkey warriors fight demons
in the Battle of Lanka.*

*(Top) The eastern section of the south gallery concerns the judgment
of the dead and their rewards or punishments. With ropes around their necks,
the damned are led to hell, Vaitaranidani. The tortures that await
include starvation, beatings with clubs, and
assault by elephants.*

*(Above) In the south gallery, a nobleman is carried by slaves
in the king's procession.*

*Suryavarman II ruled at the peak
of Khmer power and influence.
Carvings of the mighty Khmer army and
his royal processions sweep across
the western wing of the south gallery.
Traces of original gold leaf remain
on a scene of two men riding horses.*

The apsaras *embody the Khmer ideal of beauty and grace.*
Many of the traditional dance movements and poses lost during Cambodia's civil war
have been re-created from bas-reliefs.

The celestial dancers, apsaras—*nymph goddesses produced from the foam of the Churning of the Sea of Milk, the Hindu myth of creation—are carved into the walls of Angkor in more than 1,700 places. Each has her own hair ornaments, jewelry, costume, and individual characteristics.*

When Cambodia converted to Theravada Buddhism in the fourteenth century,
Angkor Wat was filled with statues of the Buddha.
One of the cruciform galleries became the Hall of a Thousand Buddhas,
and the vestibules of the central sanctuary were
turned into shrines.

Opposite: Angkor Wat has been a place of pilgrimage,
worshiped since its inception.

On the far side of the
laterite fourth enclosure wall,
a moat measuring almost a mile (1.5 km)
on each side lined with
sandstone embankments forms the
external boundary of the temple.
The total area encompasses
an enormous 494 acres (200 hectares).

PHNOM
BAKHENG

*Phnom Bakheng was at the center
of the first capital of Angkor,
Yasodharapura, circa 907.
The huge sandstone and laterite
temple mountain was carved
into the bedrock at the
top of one of the most strategic
promontories in the area.*

*Top: The architectural plan of Phnom Bakheng, a precursor to Angkor Wat,
incorporates astronomical measurements and symbolic numbers, creating a sacred mandala,
a building that represents Mount Meru as well as functioning as a ritual calendar.*

*Above: Forty-four brick towers are arranged around the base of Phnom Bakheng,
while sixty smaller sandstone prasat towers adorn its steep axial stairways.
Five terraces lead to the summit, which is crowned with a quincunx of sandstone towers.*

*Opposite: An image of the devaraja Yasodharesvara
was in the central sanctuary. The four surrounding shrines housed lingas and were
decorated with devatas and foliated scrolls.*

BAKSEI
CHAMKRONG

This miniature temple mountain
is located at the foot of Phnom Bakheng.
The pyramid is made of laterite,
topped by a single brick tower on a
sandstone base.
Originally Baksei Chamkrong
contained a golden image of Shiva.

ANGKOR
THOM

SOUTH
GOPURA

The main entrance to Angkor Thom
was the Southern Causeway,
which was lined by colossal statues of
108 mythical beings, 54 on each side.

*The road from Angkor Wat to the Bayon temple at the center
of the royal city of Angkor Thom passed through the southern gopura.
The royal city is divided into equal quarters,
with grand entrances from the cardinal directions.*

*The causeway symbolizes a "rainbow bridge,"
a link between the mundane world of humans and the
sacred world of the gods.*

NORTH
GOPURA

The entry towers are similar in design.
Each is seventy-five feet (23 m) high,
and surmounted by four heads,
which face toward the cardinal directions.

VICTORY GATE AND GATE OF DEATH

There are two gopuras *on the eastern side:*
the Victory Gate (opposite), which led from the east directly to the Royal Enclosure,
where the palace stood, and the Gate of Death (above).
These gates could originally be secured by huge wooden doors.

ELEPHANT
TERRACE

*Lavish wooden buildings probably
stood on the Elephant Terrace,
from which the king could
review processions and ritual celebrations.
Three large and two smaller stairways
project east into the Royal Square.*

*The thousand-foot (300 m) Elephant Terrace extends from
the enclosure wall near the Baphuon to the Royal Terrace.
The two levels are decorated with* naga *balustrades,* garudas, *and
lion-headed figures.*

Top: Adjacent to the Elephant Terrace is an
excavated structure that pre-dates it.
An inner wall is finely carved with mythological figures,
the most famous of which is a horse with five heads.

Above: Other sections of the terrace show
sculpted friezes of hunting scenes, in which life-size
elephants are mounted by mahouts.

ROYAL
TERRACE

*The Royal Terrace, constructed
in the late twelfth century,
is lavishly illustrated with images
of the king, queen, and princesses.*

*Below:
A statue sitting on the Royal Terrace,
known as "the Leper King"
because it is mottled with lichen,
is now believed to represent Yama,
or Dharmaraja,
assessor of the underworld.
The terrace was likely the location
of the royal crematorium.*

The Royal Terrace's present configuration is curious,
combining several structures from different eras. During construction
a section appears to have been filled with rubble,
preserving the carvings from the elements until its renovation
in 1911 by the French.

Interior walls of the terrace are ornately carved with bas-reliefs.
Multiple registers portray mythological inhabitants
of Mount Meru—divinities above, and deities of the
underworld below.

BAPHUON

The beauty and monumental size of Udayadityavarman II's
"Golden Mountain" was legendary. The eleventh-century Baphuon was once
a massive five-tiered pyramid, raised atop an earthen mound.
Since 1908 the French have been restoring the site, and the only sections
currently accessible are the causeway and some of the bas-reliefs.
The four doors of the east gopura of the upper terrace
are carved with scenes from Hindu epics.

PHIMEANAKAS AND THE ROYAL POND

Phimeanakas is the only building extant in the walled
Royal Enclosure. A mere shell remains of the three-tiered pyramid built
first as a state temple in the late tenth century, which became
the royal chapel of Jayavarman V.

*The king slept on the top level of the temple mountain and,
according to legend, copulated each night with a nine-headed serpent in
the form of a woman. The destinies of the king and the realm
were tied to this assignation. On the summit are the remains of a
single cruciform sanctuary, surrounded by galleries.*

*Within the Royal Enclosure are five sras, the largest of which
is faced with sandstone and surrounded by a two-tiered terrace,
carved with bas-reliefs.*

PREAH PALILAY

*In the northwest corner of Angkor Thom, within a forest of
silk-cotton trees (Ceiba pentandra), sits the twelfth-century Buddhist shrine
of Preah Palilay, a single sandstone tower with porches set upon
a steep terraced base.*

TEP PRANAM

Top: North of the Royal Terrace lies the ninth-century
Buddhist cruciform terrace of Tep Pranam.
Two large Buddhas, destroyed during the civil war, have been
reassembled and reinstalled in recent times.

Above: A sandstone pediment, once part of the thirteenth-century gopura,
portrays the legend of the temptation of the Buddha.
Mara, goddess of physical desire, accompanied by demons,
attacks the Buddha in an effort to prevent him from
reaching enlightenment.

PREAH
PITHU

The five similar temples of
the Preah Pithu group each had
a single sanctuary tower
set upon a high terraced base.
Temple T, shown here,
and three others were Brahmanic,
with lingas inside,
and were constructed in the
thirteenth century.

PRASAT SUOR PRAT

*Above and opposite: The twelve laterite towers
of Prasat Suor Prat stand in a line facing the terraces,
on either side of the Gate of Victory avenue.
Scholars suggest that they were used for viewing
pageants and ceremonies.*

NORTH KLEANG

Since the Kleangs are without sanctuaries or towers, they may have been
used for the reception of dignitaries. Built by Jayavarman V
in the late tenth century, the North Kleang is older, with fine workmanship
and detail; the south is unfinished.

SOUTH KLEANG

The galleries are made of massive sandstone blocks,
set on molded base platforms.
Their thick walls are decorated at the base and cornice and
pierced by huge balustered windows.

BAYON

*In the late twelfth century,
a hundred years after the construction
of Angkor Wat,
Jayavarman VII built his state temple
at the center of the royal city
of Angkor Thom.
This extraordinary structure
was created and modified over centuries,
resulting in a complex assembly
of towers, galleries, and stairways.*

Above: The structure of Bayon represents a microcosm of the
mythological cosmos similar to Borobudur in Java.
It is an architectural hybrid of a Meru shrine and a stupa, in which the pilgrim
circles and ascends the monument simultaneously, to end on a
top platform, open to the sky, in the presence of the deities.
The central sanctuary is surrounded by a circular paved walkway,
a pradakshina, for circumnabulation of
the symbolic mountain.

Opposite: Taking into account the enclosure walls it shared with
Angkor Thom, the Bayon had four enclosures; it also shared
Angkor Thom's moat. The brilliant design was hastily built over previous temples;
flaws in its construction, such as the lack of a deep foundation,
have necessitated modification when towers collapsed,
or an area had to be raised.

*Above and opposite: Of the original forty-nine towers,
more than thirty-five still stand, carved with over two hundred
colossal faces. They represent the Bodhisattava of compassion,
Avalokitesvara, also known as Lokesvara, who projects
Buddha consciousness to the cardinal directions.
But by also being modeled upon Jayavarman VII, the king
becomes the god thereby expanding his power
throughout the universe.*

*In a bas-relief on a gallery outer wall,
a naval battle ensues between
the Cham warriors and the Khmer
on Tonle Sap Lake.
Ropes are thrown from one ship to
another as an attempt is made
to board the enemy ship,
while a crocodile eats a fallen warrior.
The lower register shows scenes
of daily life.*

Above: Two concentric galleries are covered with some of the
best bas-reliefs in Khmer art, created over two eras.
The vivid, richly detailed portraits of military engagements,
processions, and daily life are more deeply cut
than at Angkor Wat.

Above and opposite top:
The Bayon was dedicated as a Mahayana Buddhist shrine
with a large Buddha inside the central sanctuary.
However, inscriptions on the doorjambs indicate that
some of the face towers were also used as shrines
to earlier Brahmanic deities, such as Shiva, represented by
this linga, and Vishnu.

THE SIGNIFICANCE
OF THE CALENDAR AT ANGKOR WAT

Eleanor Mannikka

No documents survive on Khmer temple architecture from the Angkor period, but the *Silpa Prakasa,* an eleventh-century architectural text from Orissa in northeast India, tells us that a Hindu temple must be constructed in harmony with the movements of the sun, moon, and planets. Angkor Wat may be Buddhist now, but it was originally a Hindu temple constructed in the twelfth century by priest-architects who had inherited a good part of their religion and their architectural tradition from India. Typically, these cycles of time include divisions like those of a day, a lunar half-month, a solar month, or a lunar year. Two such cycles—the 365.24 days in a solar year and the 354.36 days in a lunar year—are sacred aspects of the sun god Surya and the lunar god Chandra, respectively. These cycles and other numerical attributes of the gods are as much a part of Angkor Wat's consecrated precincts as any solid image.

Perhaps calendrical cycles have always carried a divine aura, representing as they do seemingly unchanging, repetitive periods in a world that is otherwise abjectly impermanent. Tracked by astronomer-priests, celebrated by recurring holy days, the many reliable, steady time cycles in a Hindu calendar have cast a sacred glow around the simple passage of time. Much like the multiple movements of the earth through space as it rotates, wobbles, and orbits the sun, multiple time cycles overlap. At any given moment we can define the time in terms of the hour, the day, the phase of the moon, the month, or the year. Hindu time periods range far beyond that of a year into much larger megacycles. Calendrical representations in the measurements of Angkor Wat, similarly, overlap each other, yet still clearly define each segment of the temple.

A Hindu temple may mirror our vision of the infinite universe, but it must also bring the gods down to Earth, anchoring them within hallowed chambers and open courtyards. It is the presence of divinity that transformed Angkor Wat into a sacrosanct space and facilitated a desired union between worshiper and worshiped. Exactly how the gods could be persuaded to grace Angkor Wat and other Khmer temples with their presence was once the substance of priestly architectural texts, long since turned to dust.

The stone statues of Hindu gods in Cambodia were named after ancestors, with a suffix to indicate their divine identity; by these names alone, an ancestor and an image were joined. The statue may have looked like Vishnu or Shiva or Lakshmi and may have had multiple arms or a third eye, or carried attributes like a trident or conch shell to identify it, but its clothing was the clothing of Khmer royalty, and as well as possessing an ancestor's name, it may have

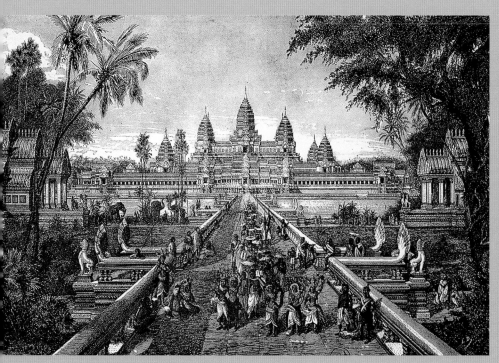

hograph by Louis Delaporte showing the western entrance to Angkor Wat. Published in 1880.

borne the features of that ancestor — or even those of the living king. By bringing the image of a divinity into the temple, Khmer priests also invoked the ancestors. This is a subtle, conceptually elusive combination, a sublime union that blessed Angkor's temples with a continually vital and contemporary spiritual presence.

Along with the soaring towers and delicate bas-reliefs, measurements inspired by the calendar were offerings to the gods, a way of giving them the best and most accurate cosmological setting, just as an honored guest is offered the best seat in the house. Because of the sacred quality of numbers that define divinity, measurements were an important means of bringing the gods and their ancestral components to Angkor Wat.

One might say that a union with the sun god begins to happen the moment a devotee enters any numerically charged solar space. Nowhere is that union more profound and far-reaching than in the central sanctuary of Angkor Wat, where in the holiest of holy chambers, the king himself would be joined with Vishnu, chief of all solar gods, in a sublime melding of the divine-human interface. The central tower of Angkor Wat, visible from a great distance, represented the heart of the king's extensive domains. It was at once the symbolic center of the nation and the actual center where secular and sacred power joined forces. From that unparalleled space, Vishnu and the king ruled over the Khmer people.

In that same space, the image of Vishnu was once located with astounding accuracy right at the latitude of Angkor Wat. The north-south axis of the central sanctuary measures 13.43 cubits (about 20 feet [6 m]), while the latitude of Angkor Wat is 13.41 degrees north. (A cubit, defined as the length between the elbow and the fingertips, would at Angkor Wat have been determined by the body of the king.) Although a very slight discrepancy exists between the latitude measurement in the sanctuary and that of the temple, the architect's intent is clear. That the length of 13.43 cubits was used as a standard of measure in the second or middle gallery in particular indicates that it was anything but a random number. In the central sanctuary, Vishnu is not only placed at the latitude of Angkor Wat, he is also placed along the axis of the earth.

The builders of Angkor knew the earth was round. They inherited that knowledge from Indian astronomers, who in the sixth century described the earth as being like an iron ball suspended in space between two magnets. This knowledge is reflected in Hindu cosmology and was passed on to the Khmers, who were to build it into the central tower of Angkor Wat.

The tower that rises above the ceiling of the central sanctuary is 54 cubits high, to the top of its now missing finial. The shaft that once went down from the floor of the sanctuary to the sacred objects buried when construction began also measures 54 cubits, or 80 feet (25 m), in length. In the Khmer cosmological system, uniquely, fifty-four gods live at the north celestial pole, and fifty-four antigods live at the south celestial pole.

Finally, by putting the statue at the center of a 13.43-cubit north-south axis, the architects have brought their cosmic configuration to the latitude of Angkor Wat. Vishnu is very precisely placed on that round ball floating in space, with the ecliptic around him and the gods and antigods above and below his earthly temple abode. As a supreme offering to Vishnu who would rule all others from this site, the central sanctuary of Angkor Wat could not have been a more perfect home.

The temple is linked to the gods in the heavens in other ways. During the long and clear Cambodian nights, when the stars filled every inch of the black sky, the astronomer-priests stood on the long western causeway leading straight to the heart of Angkor Wat and recorded the movements of the moon against the towers in the top two galleries of the temple. The causeway has six sets of staircases paired across from each other at regular intervals over a distance of 1,140 feet (342 m). If one stands exactly along the central line of the causeway at the first five sets of staircases in succession, there are a total of twelve lunar alignments with the towers. Eight alignments are with the towers of the middle gallery, a gallery whose measurements are only lunar or lunar-related.

The same is true of the western causeway. Its measurements are not solar but lunar in meaning. In this perfect temple, the astronomers stood on a lunar causeway, watching the moon rise over lunar towers.

But in spite of recurrent lunar symbolism, Angkor Wat is, after all, dedicated to Vishnu. The king who constructed the temple took the name of Suryavarman—"protected by Surya, the sun." On the day of the spring equinox around March 21 each year, the sun rises directly over the central tower of Angkor Wat when observed from the top of the first northern staircase along the causeway. Three days later the sun rises directly over the central tower once again, when observed from the center of the causeway, exactly in front of the staircase. One can imagine the masses of people gathering in the dark predawn hours of the spring equinox day, crowding into the courtyard in front of the main western entrance. Rituals would have been performed, accompanied by music and drumming, and most likely court dances as well. When the sun rose over the central tower at 6:35 A.M.—long after it was light—it would look as though the god Vishnu inside the tower were sending forth Surya to begin a new calendar year.

Since the king and Vishnu were inextricably joined in spiritual union in the central tower of Angkor Wat, the king himself shared in some of Vishnu's solar glory. For three days the Khmers celebrated their new year with the final closure on the third day, the day that began with the sun rising over the central tower for the second and last time.

The second or middle gallery of Angkor Wat, with all its lunar-related measurements, is dedicated not only to Chandra, the god of the moon, but also to Brahma, another form of Vishnu. In one Hindu creation myth, Vishnu lies asleep on the Milky Ocean—the Milky Way—and as his consort Lakshmi delicately strokes his lower leg, he awakens from his slumber and sends a lotus stalk upward from his navel. At the top of the stalk he manifests as Brahma, a four-headed deity who then creates time and space. This moment is immortalized in countless images and bas-reliefs from Hindu temples stretching all the way from India to Cambodia and beyond. For reasons that are lost in the misty reaches of ancient history, the lotus stalk that supports Brahma came to be identified as the axis of the earth in Cambodia, an axis that extends up toward Brahma at the north celestial pole and down to the antigods at the south celestial pole. If we search for Brahma in the night sky when the north celestial pole is visible, we can more or less identify him with Polaris, the North Star. At the same time, all the stars in the universe appear to circle the north celestial pole in a counterclockwise direction. So whether or not any particular star is at this hub, the location of Brahma is still apparent for all to see.

Vishnu, who rests in the central sanctuary of Angkor Wat, is not only a solar god sending forth the sun each year, but also the lunar Brahma, his emanation that created all of time and space, which makes Vishnu a supreme ruler over the diurnal and nocturnal skies, just as Suryavarman once ruled supreme over a multifaceted nation. From a Khmer perspective, Vishnu and Suryavarman were ritually and symbolically joined in the central tower of Angkor Wat, where they reigned over the heavenly and human realms in harmony.

The tower is at the hub of the squared-off upper elevation and can be approached from any one of twelve staircases, three on a side. These twelve staircases are symbols of the twelve solar months, divided into three months each between the four equinox and solstice days. If the architecture of the temple were mobile, we could envision the twelve staircases revolving around the central sanctuary like the solar zodiac signs; the sun itself would appear to revolve around Brahma at the north celestial pole.

As the king approached the central tower of Angkor Wat to pay homage to Vishnu, he would have first passed through the lunar middle gallery and completed his homage to Brahma. In philosophical terms, this has tremendous import: since Brahma is the creator of time and space, the king and his priests would ascend to the level of the creator in the lunar middle gallery, and then go beyond him—beyond time and space itself—into the presence of Vishnu in the central sanctuary.

In his aspect as supreme deity, Vishnu is not bounded by conceptual constraints of cyclical time or three-dimensional space. The union of the king and Vishnu in the central sanctuary would have occurred in a consecrated space that lay outside the world as we know it. From the perspective of the Supreme Vishnu, that space would have been beyond our three-dimensional world, but from our perspective, the central tower represents the earth and the celestial realm, seen from our planet.

Another great change happens before the king or his priests reach the lunar middle gallery. They pass through their own realm in the third, or outermost, gallery in the set of three at the heart of the temple complex. The third gallery, which is dedicated to the king, is one of the most photographed of spaces because of the spectacular, seemingly endless sequence of bas-reliefs that enliven its interior wall. These reliefs begin on the west as one enters and turns to the right, and continue all the way around an encircling corridor that runs for an astounding 2,427 feet (740 m).

On the south side of this gallery King Suryavarman II is depicted twice in person: once receiving homage from his main ministers after an obvious victory in battle (almost unique in his reign), and once joining his ministers in a heraldic victory procession. It is likely that the rest of the original reliefs in this gallery also alludes to the history of the king, as it is possible to see logical connections to the king's own exploits in the legends they depict.

Because of the figures of King Suryavarman, this gallery has in the literature always been referred to as the "historical gallery." We are at least partially in the mundane world at this level of Angkor Wat, a world apparently defined by the king and his ministers. We can look through the widely spaced columns along the corridors and gaze outward at the vast space of the broad, open courtyard and beyond, to the tops of the distant trees, or we can gaze inward at the stories told along the walls and join the king and the gods in our stroll through history and legend.

By the sixth century at the very least, Indian astronomers were working with a 360-degree circle. Assyro-Babylonian civilizations created a system of twenty-four hours in one day with sixty minutes in an hour and sixty seconds in a minute. Both time and space, then, have the same essential units of measure—sixty seconds in each of sixty minutes that make up either one degree or one hour, both in a system regulated by multiples of 10 or 12. Even more astounding is a little-noted fact: the Mesopotamian measurements of time and space contain the numbers of three of the four major Hindu time cycles, excluding the Golden Age. To put this succinctly, there are 432,000 seconds in a 120-degree circle, 864,000 seconds in a 240-degree circle, and 1,296,000 seconds in a 360-degree circle. The three eras that followed each other once the Golden Age ended have lengths of 1,296,000, 864,000, and 432,000 years.

What do all these numbers mean? For one thing, it would appear that the earliest Indian astronomy and astronomy in the ancient Middle East are somehow related. Even more compelling is the interchangeability of the base units of time and space measurements, a key philosophical aspect of the measurement systems of Angkor Wat. Perhaps the architects of Angkor Wat were aware of these base units and their implications. The outermost border of Angkor Wat, the border that circles the outer edge of the moat, is 120 units in circumference and 60 units along its north-south and east-west axes combined. These large units of measurement are based on a module of 108 cubits, 108 being one of the most sacred numbers in all of Asia, to Hindus and Buddhists alike. In Cambodia, this may have been the reason for the total of 108 gods and antigods at the north and south celestial poles. If the entire cosmological and calendrical systems of Angkor Wat are encompassed by and based on the numbers 120 (12 x 10) in the circumference and 60 along the axes of the temple, then the Khmer architects must have regarded these two numbers with special veneration, especially since their module is 108 cubits.

The architects would have been familiar with the sixty-minute, sixty-second divisions of the degrees in a circle, and it seems hard to believe they would not have known the connections between the seconds in a circle and the Hindu time periods. But we will never know for sure. Sadly, the knowledge that built Angkor Wat and its fascinating systems of measurement and astronomical observation has long since disappeared. Khmer and Indian architects guarded their secrets by maintaining an oral tradition that was handed down from master to disciple. When stone temple building stopped at Angkor in the thirteenth century, the oral tradition of the architects had no reason to continue.

By the fifteenth century, when the site was abandoned and the focus of government moved far to the south, the ancient architectural texts had disappeared, victims of the passage of time and of an unrelenting subtropical climate. The secrets of seven hundred years of Khmer temple construction had been lost within a century or two at the most. At the end of the nineteenth century, French scholars had begun to translate an enormous body of ancient Khmer stone inscriptions. These records of genealogies and history, land boundaries and temple consecrations, were found almost at every turn.

The inscriptions make it clear that Khmer temple architects were not only priests but astronomers as well. The position of the sun, moon, and sometimes all of the visible planets against the backdrop of constellations was elaborated in great detail at the beginning of many of these inscriptions. The exact day in the lunar cycle was often stated precisely; "the third day of the waxing moon" of a particular lunar half-month, for example. These descriptions are so precise that today astronomers can turn back the celestial clock to the exact day and date ascribed to a certain event. Astronomy was an essential component of priestly knowledge.

The twentieth century was a time of discovery and reckoning at Angkor, as sculptural styles were defined and art and architecture put into an accurate chronological sequence. Now, at the dawn of the twenty-first century, we are hopefully closer to the secrets of twelfth-century Angkor Wat than ever before.

THE TEMPLES
SURROUNDING
ANGKOR

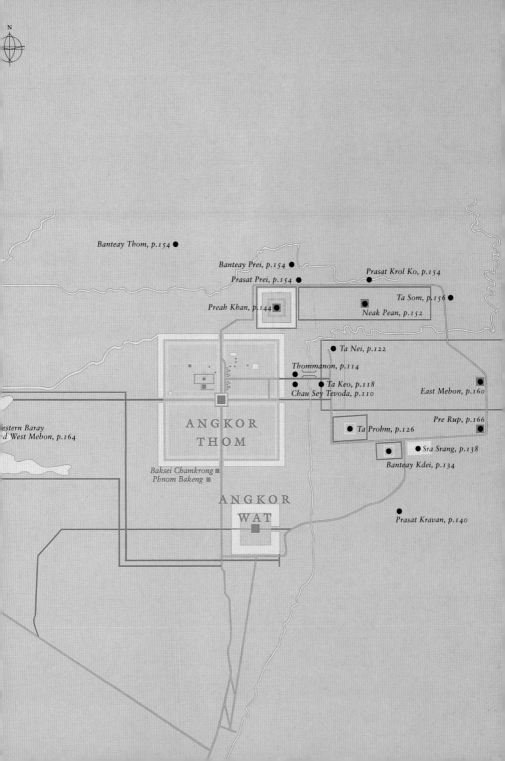

N

CHAU SAY
TEVODA

*East of the Gate of Victory
stands a pair of similarly designed shrines,
Chau Say Tevoda to the south,
and Thommanon to the north.
Built by Suryavarman II
in the mid-twelfth century, during
the classic period of Khmer art,
Chau Say Tevoda was
constructed after Thommanon
and is more elaborate.*

The ornamentation with devatas, floral patterns,
and inscribed doors is very fine, especially on the sanctuary.
Chau Say Tevoda had one of the first naga balustrades
at Angkor.

*A laterite enclosure wall with four gopuras surrounds
two libraries and a sanctuary tower.
Although enclosed by stone, the interior wooden beams
used in the original construction have deteriorated
contributing to the collapse of the buildings.*

THOMMANON

*Surrounded by the remains of
a laterite enclosure wall with two gopuras,
the east-facing sanctuary on a high,
sculpted base is topped with a four-tiered tower.
The attached mandapa has a stone roof
carved to mimic tiles.
The frontons depict scenes from
the Ramayana.*

Thommanon is believed to have been dedicated to Vishnu,
although a linga was also discovered inside.
The shrine was restored in the 1960s by Bernard-Philippe Groslier.

*The numerous, elaborately dressed devatas are nearly life-size,
with exquisitely detailed faces and headdresses.*

TA KEO

*Begun in the late tenth century,
Ta Keo was the first temple mountain
built entirely of
massive blocks of sandstone,
an impressive giant even in its unfinished state.
The temple was surrounded
by a moat, crossed by an eastern causeway,
which has boundary stones
still in place.*

*Below: Fragments of lingas and statues,
such as this eleventh-century
masculine divinity,
were found on the summit platform.*

Top: Ta Keo was constructed on three levels, with stairways
on the principal axes, topped by a quincunx of towers.

Above: The galleries surrounding the summit are similar
to those at Phimeanakas, which was built by Jayavarman V
during the same period.

*Each of the sanctuaries at Ta Keo was cruciform,
entered from four directions through vestibules,
a new development in Khmer architecture. The central sanctuary
sits sixteen feet (4.8 m) above the summit terrace.*

TA NEI

*Situated in a beautiful forest,
Ta Nei has an air of tranquillity
and mystery.
The site has only recently been cleared,
with restoration by
the Angkor Conservancy imminent.
The Buddhist shrine was
built by Jayavarman VII in the
late twelfth century.*

Top: Ta Nei's concentric enclosures consist of two long basins
on the north and south, a laterite wall, and a galleried inner enclosure.
A cruciform sanctuary with four porches is situated in the center.

Above: The courtyard at Ta Nei is filled with stones from
collapsed gopuras, galleries, and a library. The gopuras have barrel-shaped
vaulted roofs and are decorated with devatas and
false windows with balusters.

Opposite: The doorways are richly carved with floral patterns,
overgrown with moss and lichen.

TA PROHM

*Built in the late twelfth century
by Jayavarman VII,
Ta Prohm was the center of the
royal city of Rajavihara.
Both a Buddhist temple and
a monastery, it was one of
the largest monuments of the
Khmer civilization.*

*Within the 148-acre (60 hectare) grounds,
the imposing temple complex is built on a single level
covering two and a half acres (1 hectare).
The inscription states that there were 12,640 people
in residence, and details the ample treasury of gold, silk,
gems, and 260 statues of the gods.*

Top: Ta Prohm contains thirty-nine towers,
many freestanding, with carvings of dvarapalas
guarding the doors.

Above: Many small chapels are found within the temple,
such as this shrine dedicated to the brother
of Jayavarman VII, Jayakirideva.

The inner enclosure walls are intricately decorated with scrolls,
foliage patterns, devotees in prayer, and devatas.
Roots of a silk-cotton tree (Ceiba pentandra) overlaid by a
strangler fig (Ficus religiosa) must be carefully controlled,
the destruction caused by their ever-increasing weight measured
against the grip of the tangled roots that now hold
the stones in place.

Opposite: Carved above the doorways are key scenes from the life
of Siddhartha Gautama, as well as stories of the twenty-four Buddhas
preceding him, known as the Buddhavamsa Jatakas.

*Top and above: The temple has been deliberately left in
a derelict condition to fulfill the romantic expectations of visitors
who want to see the monument in the condition in which
it was originally found.*

*Top: Lintels are often hard to examine closely,
except by climbing up onto treacherous rooftops where shafts of light
penetrate the dense forest, illuminating the rare artwork.*

*Above: One of the most famous pediments at Angkor
recounts* The Great Departure, *the story of the young Buddha,
Siddhartha Gautama, leaving his father's palace at night.
Divinities muffle the horse's hooves, allowing him to slip away
without awakening the household.*

BANTEAY KDEI

The Mahayana Buddhist temple
of Banteay Kdei was constructed
in the late twelfth century
over the ruins of a tenth-century shrine
by the great Jayavarman VII,
builder of Ta Prohm and Preah Khan.
The temple-palace has a moat
paved with sandstone,
which surrounds the second enclosure.

Top: *The western approach to Banteay Kdei passes through*
a gopura *and over a causeway leading to two galleried enclosures.*

Above: *A Buddha in the middle enclosure* gopura *is actively worshiped,*
as evidenced by many offerings and the burning of incense.

Opposite: *The inner enclosure wall, which has four corner towers,*
surrounds a sanctuary and two libraries.

SRA SRANG

The royal bathing pool has
retained water for more than ten centuries.
A cruciform terrace of sandstone,
built upon a laterite foundation, is adorned
with garudas *mounting three-headed* nagas;
lions guard the steps leading down
to the water. An inscription expressly forbids
the washing of elephants here,
which would damage the pool's
delicate sandstone lining.

PRASAT
KRAVAN

*An inscription records
the dedication date as 921,
placing Prasat Kravan as
a contemporary of Phnom Bakheng.
Five temples constructed of
sandstone and brick
sit upon a common base, facing east.
The center and north towers
contain sculpted brick bas-reliefs
bearing traces of stucco.*

The interior of the central tower is an homage to Vishnu.
The west wall (center) shows Vishnu with six rows of
attendants; the north wall portrays Vishnu on the shoulders
of a garuda; on the south wall, Vishnu
crosses the cosmic ocean, carrying his four attributes.
A square pedestal in the center once held a linga.

*The interior of the north tower portrays
Lakshmi, Vishnu's four-armed consort, with two attendants
kneeling in reverence. The unusual carved brick reliefs
are found nowhere else at Angkor.*

PREAH
KHAN

*At the end of the twelfth century,
Jayavarman VII built not only
a Buddhist shrine
but the royal city of Nagarajayacri.
Within its precincts was a monastery,
a university, shrines to
Shiva, Vishnu, and the ancestors,
and possibly a palace.*

*Top: This two-story pavillion with round columns is unique
in Khmer architecture. The* preah khan, *or sacred sword,
symbol of the power and sovereignty of the* devaraja *was believed
to have been kept inside.*

*Above: The third enclosure, containing the two-story building
and paved walkway with raised* naga *balustrades can be viewed
from a vaulted roof.*

Top: *Preah Khan is only slightly smaller than Ta Prohm, which was*
also built, five years earlier, by Jayavarman VII.
The central sanctuary roofs have the rounded outlines
of Buddhist stupas.

Above: *Unlike a temple mountain, Preah Khan is constructed on*
a single level spread out over 140 acres (57 hectares).
The complex arrangement of shrines includes towered porticos and
interconnected galleries. This view of the northern section
of the second enclosure shows the prasat *of a Shiva sanctuary.*

Top: *Four courtyards, each with twenty-four pillars, define the cruciform shape of the Hall of Dancers. The roof was a corbeled vault of nearly twenty feet (6 m), the largest span at Angkor.*

Above: *A carving of the third enclosure wall depicts a* devata *between false windows with balustrades. Niches throughout the temple previously held images of the Buddha.*

According to an inscription from 1911, more than one thousand dancers once performed and lived at Preah Khan.

*Left: Boundary stones at the east entrance featured a mythical creature
with a human torso, the legs of a garuda, and a lion's face.*

*Right: The eastern causeway is lined with a balustrade
of colossal deities holding the body of a naga.*

*Opposite: Seventy-two giant garudas holding nagas in their claws
protect the two-mile (3 km) outer enclosure wall.*

NEAK
PEAN

*In the middle of the baray of Preah Khan
is an island that has a pond
with a tower in the center. Dedicated to
Avalokitesvara, it represents
Anavatapta, a mythical lake reputed
to cure all illness.*

*Below: Within the east chapel
is a sculpted fountainhead,
considered an oracle. Water from the pond
is poured into it and flows
out of its mouth.*

BANTEAY PREI

*Top right: Once surrounded by
a moat, the east-facing sanctuary
still stands; many of its carved
devatas, dvarapalas, and false windows
with balusters are still intact.
A low vaulted gallery, surrounds the
courtyard, which is filled with
stones from the collapsed gopuras.*

BANTEAY THOM

*Top far right: The entrance is strewn
with remnants of a gopura, which retains
a vaulted roof and carved dvarapala
standing beside the doorways.
A miniature shrine antefix has fallen
from one of the towers. Behind
the gopura the overgrown courtyard
contains three towers in a line and
two collapsed libraries.*

PRASAT KROL KO

*Bottom right: The partially ruined
east gopura has octagonal colonettes,
foliated carvings, and false windows
with balusters. Behind it are the
east-facing cruciform sanctuary and
a library. The courtyard contains
pediments awaiting renovation.*

PRASAT PREI

*Bottom far right: In the late twelfth
through the early thirteenth centuries,
Jayavarman VII constructed several
small Buddhist shrines northeast
of Angkor Thom and Preah Khan.
The remains of an enclosure wall and
a gopura lie in front of
the partially restored sanctuary
of Prasat Prei.*

TA SOM

*The Buddhist shrine of Ta Som,
built in the late twelfth century
by Jayavarman VII, has similarities
to Preah Khan, although it is
much smaller. The east gopura
of the middle enclosure is engulfed
by a strangler fig tree.*

Top: Ta Som has three concentric enclosures,
defined by two walls, which are separated by a moat.
The central sanctuary is enclosed by a gallery
with four corner towers.

Above: Lining the walls of the galleries of the
inner courtyard are carvings of devatas, foliated scrolls, and
decorative false windows with lowered blinds.

Opposite: The face of Avelokesvara
looks to the cardinal directions on the gopura towers
of the east and west entrances.
The central Buddhist figure of the gopura was removed
during the time of the thirteenth-century
Brahmanic orthodoxy.

EAST
MEBON

When the East Mebon was dedicated to
Shiva and Parvati in 953,
the water of the Yasodharatataka, or
East Baray, surrounded the temple.
Only the sandstone pillars remain of the
second enclosure galleries, which were
probably used for meditation.

Below: The god Ganesha was in residence
at the end of the tenth century.

Top: The three-tiered pyramid has a quincunx of towers
upon a summit platform, surrounded by eight subsidiary brick towers.
The Central Sanctuary held the royal linga, Rajendrasvara.

Above: Elephants found on the corners of terraces of both enclosures are
carved from a single piece of stone.

Opposite: Stone lion guardians cast shadows upon the ornately carved
false doors of a secondary brick tower.
The inscription is unusual in that it mentions the royal architect,
Kavindrarimathana, by name.

WESTERN
BARAY
AND
WEST MEBON

Udayadityavarman I built Angkor's largest artificial lake, which has continued to hold water for almost a thousand years. Only a vestige remains of the western Mebon temple, situated on an island in the lake's center.

Below: An enormous reclining Vishnu with four arms was rediscovered in 1936, its location revealed through the dream of a local worker. The eleventh-century bronze was once gilded and set with precious stones.

PRE RUP

*Rajendravarman II constructed
Pre Rup in the second half of
the tenth century as his state temple
and the center of a royal city.
The classic three-tiered pyramid
is surrounded by two enclosure walls.*

Top: The eastern entrance passes through a cruciform gopura.
and opens into the second enclosure. The summit pyramid
has twelve small prasat towers on the lower level.
The four corner towers on the top platform contained images of Vishnu,
Shiva and their consorts Lakshmi and Uma.

Above: Crumbling remains of pillared galleries with balustered
windows surround the temple mountain.

Opposite: The Central Sanctuary opens to the east, with false doors
on its sides. Pairs of sculpted lions guard the stairways,
and remnants of stucco decoration cling to the brick walls.

THE ARCHITECTURE
AND CONSERVATION OF ANGKOR

John Sanday

T he architecture of Angkor has inspired architects, artists, travelers, and dreamers from around the world. Those who have discovered this unrivaled group of monuments have fulfilled a dream. As they wander through the sites, most visitors would like to know how these mighty structures were built, where the materials came from, and how were they conceived.

Perhaps one of the easiest ways to begin to understand the architecture is to look at Angkor through the eyes of the local foreman builder, who would have been working as a member of the palace retinue and would have been in charge of building the Khmer king's palaces and temples. At its pinnacle of development, Angkor would have had a program of continuous construction under way. These temples were major construction sites, using thousands of workers, hundreds of elephants, and enormous quantities of materials such as sandstone and laterite. There were great technical demands in designs for the temple structures, which were faultlessly located, possibly using astrology or a magnetic compass. Recent bearings show the structures to be placed on an exact east-west compass bearing with a variation of 4 degrees from true north. Construction and management of the exceptional hydrological systems posed the challenge of making full use of the assets provided by the Tonle Sap, or "great lake," which was the most likely influence on the location of this great Khmer empire. (See Goodman essay, p. 256.)

The challenge we face today is to understand how and why these great structures were created and constructed with such limited equipment. In my endeavors to conserve and repair Preah Khan, we have consciously limited our use of modern equipment, first to keep the project's running costs low, and second, to make use of the traditional skills instinctive in our team of craftsmen. These restrictions have helped us comprehend in a small way how the temples of Angkor were conceived and built.

It is important to take into account the lack of building knowledge among the Khmers. Despite their great artistic skills in decorating the magnificent temples of Angkor, their skills in engineering these massive structures, combining brick and stone and timber, were limited.

Before the arrival of Indian traders in the south of present-day Cambodia, it appears that the Khmers built with wood. The domestic dwelling, for example, was a simple structure built on stilts with pitched roofs covered in palm leaves, and it is probable that early religious shrines were constructed in a similar way. As wood is an ephemeral material, these timber structures quickly disappeared in the subtropical jungles of Angkor soon after they were abandoned, so that no archaeological evidence of them has endured aboveground.

The archival materials we find in most other Asian countries are lacking in Angkor; the only records are those carved in stone on the buildings themselves. Most records were written on palm leaves and similar perishable material, which quickly became the victim of fungi and insects in the very humid climate. Historians and researchers have therefore relied on inscriptions carved on doorjambs at temple entrances or on the stelae that have been found in some of the temples. Over 1,200 inscriptions have been identified, but it is likely that many more have long since disappeared. Most of these inscriptions are now housed in the Angkor Conservancy. These inscriptions provide wonderfully evocative descriptions and long lists of donations as well as instructions on the management of the temples. There is little, however, to help present-day historians discover how the temples were laid out or constructed. The texts were written in Sanskrit or in Khmer. Sanskrit texts were usually written in verse following a fairly standard format; their eulogies of the temple founder provide interesting information about the kings. The Khmer inscriptions, by contrast, were written in prose, and most often documented the land and goods owned by the temple. These inscriptions could be construed as a roll of honor listing people who worked on or contributed to the temple's construction or establishment.

One of the best-known and most often quoted inscriptions is that of Preah Khan. Its six-foot (2 m)-high stele stood on the main axial path in Preah Khan until 1995, when fears that it would be looted prompted its removal to the safety of the Angkor Conservancy compound, a move that took over twenty workers and a large truck. The inscription tells of the location of Preah Khan, where once there was a lake of blood, referring to the great battle on the site where Jayavarman VII finally defeated the Cham, and where the Cham king died. We are also informed that there were 515 secondary deities in the shrines of Preah Khan and that there were 139 festival days. References are also made to the temple's wealth—in the quantities of gold in its treasury and the large numbers of bronze sheets used, probably to line the interior of the central shrine—and indirectly to its construction.

The question is often asked, Why are there so many temples, and for what purposes were they built? It is important to understand the development of Angkor as one of the greatest empires to have existed—a city of over a million inhabitants, ruled over by a powerful king. Each king expressed his power by constructing new edifices, creating temples of durable materials to honor the gods; in some cases the temples were built to honor the kings themselves as devarajas, "god-kings." The act of building was seen as an act of worship, and therefore each new king built his own state temple as well as a series of associated structures competing with his predecessor. Only during latter reigns were buildings recycled or added to by successors.

The sacred ground on which the temple was built represents the universe, and the temple itself, often with five towers representing five peaks, signifies the mythological Mount Meru at the center of this universe. Mount Meru thus becomes the abode of the gods, encircled by a primordial ocean. This imagery becomes clear when we study more closely the temples described as temple mountains. Two types of temple-mountain structures exist in Angkor: those constructed on real hillocks, such as Phnom Bakheng, where the complex has been carefully located on a geological outcrop, an unusual phenomenon in and around Angkor; or man-made temple mountains, of which Angkor Wat is the best example.

All temples were raised off the ground on platforms. This was a practical measure as well as a recognition of the difference between heaven and Earth, the sacred and the profane; these platforms separated the temples from the villages or the dwellings around them, where access was no doubt by elephant or bullock cart. Once on the platform, any visitor would be on foot. A large cruciform platform usually extends in front of the main entrance to the temple complex, providing a place for assembling the royal retinue. The monarch would travel toward the central shrine, possibly in a palanquin, someone carrying the "Preah Khan" or sacred sword, would lead the procession to the central shrine.

Great Processional Ways paved either in sandstone or in laterite lead up to enclosure walls surrounding the temples. Along the principal access route various individual structures have been classified by French archaeologists as either libraries or sanctuaries where Agni, the god of the sacred flame, may have been kept, or other divinities sheltered.

PERIODS OF KHMER ARCHITECTURE

Historians have categorized Khmer architecture into the pre-Angkorian period, the transitional period, and the Angkorian period. In the Angkorian period, during the flowering of the Khmer civilization, there are ten different styles, which are named after the most influential building of each style.

The architectural styles of Angkor developed over seven centuries, and in this period perhaps the most notable change was an increase in size and scale. The individual structures all retained the same profile, that of a high tower, whether it be set over a *gopura*, or gateway, or a temple shrine. The forerunners of Khmer culture were the civilizations of Chenla and Funan, the latter being based in the Mekong Delta. The people of Chenla, on the southern coastline of present-day Cambodia, were probably influenced by wealthy Indian traders and believed that copying Indian culture would bring them wealth and happiness. Hinduism was therefore introduced to the Chenla empire, and along with religious icons and beliefs came the shrines and temples in which the divinities were installed. Stylistically the shape or profile of the temple shrines is very similar to the tall tapering towers in stone and brick found in southern India. Soon after this architectural style was introduced, it was embellished in Angkor at the birth of a great empire.

It is worth making brief mention of the pre-Angkorian period (c. 610–c. 825), as this encompassed the first structures to be built at the Angkor site as we know it today. The first visible evidence of a temple compound can be seen at the eighth-century temple complex of Ak Yum. Little is known of its origins other than what is written on an inscription found when the temple was rediscovered in 1932. The temple complex was located in a .7-square-mile (2 sq km) enclosure and is said to be the first temple mountain. The temple is built on a 1,075-square-foot (100 sq m) stone base and two subsequent brick platforms. The temple mountain was crowned with a quincunx of five brick towers. When the West Baray, or reservoir, was constructed, the complex was half buried by the *baray*'s southern dike.

As we have learned in previous chapters, the transitional period (c. 825–c. 875) was established over a period of fifty years in the Kulen Hills, at which time the Kulen style was developed under Jayavarman II. The temple structures were modest in size; square towers were built of brick on a laterite base, and doorways were carved using local sandstone. All the temples of this period are in a state of ruin.

The builders of Angkor, during the Angkorian period (c. 875–c. 1243), returned to the fertile plains below the Kulen Hills to Hariharalaya, 8 miles (13 km) southeast of present-day Siem Reap. It was here that Indravarman I built the first of the great *barays* or reservoirs, known as the Indratakaka. Other than the temples, which today seem rather isolated from one another, little is left of what was once a vast empire located close to the Tonle Sap, which was originally enclosed by a large moat, part of which can still be seen. The surviving temples, known today as the Roluos group in the Preah Ko style, are the first extant structures of Angkor.

Probably as a result of flooding due to its proximity to the Tonle Sap (see Goodman essay, p. 256), Yasovarman I moved away from Hariharalaya to establish his capital around a mountain and to build his state temple, Phnom Bakheng, on the top of a natural *phnom*, or hillock. His capital was extensive, covering an area of 6 square miles (16 sq km), making it larger than that of present-day Angkor Thom. The state temple set on the summit of the hillock created the new Bakheng style and started a trend of building on other *phnom* in the vicinity, with the later construction of temples on Phnom Bok and Phnom Krom. The style copied very much that of the Bakong in Roluos, with square terraces surrounded by square-based towers. The major change was in the materials used, as sandstone became the predominant material in the most important temples.

Interest remained in creating temple mountains in honor of the gods, Pre Rup being the next example of a truly magnificent man-made temple-mountain. Its base or pyramid was built of laterite, and the shrines in quincunx on top were brick with stucco decoration. Pre Rup was undoubtedly the inspiration for the temple built on an island in the middle of the East Baray known as East Mebon, as it is similar in style without being a temple mountain.

Phimeanakas, constructed in the late tenth century as a state temple associated with the first royal palace complex, is a temple mountain paradigm. It was described by the Chinese traveler, Chou Ta-kuan (Zhou Daguan), who spent a year in Angkor in 1296–97, as having a golden tower. In the late tenth century Ta Keo then followed, a somewhat mysterious structure, as it was never finished. Today it offers clues about the often-questioned method of construction.

One of the most imposing of the temple-mountain constructions, in its time, was the Baphuon, built by Udayadityavarman II as his state temple of Yasodharapura in the middle of the eleventh century. Today it is hard to conceptualize this mammoth structure, which fell into disrepair prior to the construction of the massive reclining Buddha in the sixteenth century. Even in its ruinous state, without the central tower and the indistinct five tiers that formed the terraces below, the sense of Mount Meru is still apparent.

The best known of all the Angkorian monuments is Angkor Wat, built between 1113 and 1150. The largest religious monument in the world, Angkor Wat is a microcosm of the Hindu universe, culminating in the five peaks of Mount Meru. In the words of Claude Jacques, "It is an architectural masterpiece of fine proportions and rich in detail—the apogee of classical Khmer construction." Eleanor Mannikka has written extensively about the rationale of its construction and its cosmological significance. Its mass and grandeur leave most mortals speechless, especially when they learn that it was constructed over only thirty-seven years.

Under Jayavarman VII's influence, Buddhism made a return to the Khmer kingdom, and as a result a different, more monastic style of architecture emerged. At the end of the twelfth century temple complexes were developed and encircled by townships, such as Ta Prohm and Preah Khan, in which the principal shrine was Buddhist. However, in recognition of the state religion, a series of surrounding shrines paid homage to the Hindu sects of Shiva Vishnu and animism, or ancestor worship. The concept of Mount Meru still prevailed, but the layout was linear, with the central tower representing Mount Meru and a series of encircling enclosure walls representing the terraces around the mountain.

It was at about this time that Jayavarman VII started building Angkor Thom and the Bayon temple, setting the style that all the later monuments emulated. Angkor Thom was built over or incorporated many of the previous temples and the earlier palace compound, but centered on the Bayon. Great *gopuras*, or gateways, led into the city, and on the many towers of the Bayon carved faces bore enigmatic smiles; these were said to be in the image of their builder. Jayavarman VII established himself as the greatest of architects of the Khmer empire, but his efforts in Angkor Thom saw the end of this great architectural epoch. Later kings concentrated on the expansion or redevelopment of existing structures, especially within Angkor Thom. The Bayon went through several significant remodeling phases, producing a very confused and congested center.

Although a date of 1431 is fixed for the demise of Angkor as the state capital, little is known of conditions at that time. It is still a mystery whether Thai armies sacked Angkor or whether there was a more practical reason for the shift to the south, such as lack of water and crop failure. By most accounts Angkor's zenith was toward the end of the twelfth century, and although some new temples were constructed in the thirteenth century, the general trend was toward the slow collapse of the great empire.

ARCHITECTURAL STYLES

The earliest standing structures to be built in Angkor in the eighth century were located close to the Tonle Sap Lake and are known as the Roluos group. It is interesting to compare these structures for their size and simplicity with those of the later Angkorian period only a few centuries later, when some of the largest and grandest structures were built in tribute to the god.

The style of architecture seen in the early Angkorian temples at Preah Ko and Lolei in Roluos, in the other early brick temples of East Mebon, Prasat Kravan, and Bat Chum, and in the unique temple of Banteay Srei all follow what was typically called the *sikhara* style of South India— tapering towerlike brick structures in which a small shrine was created to honor a Hindu divinity. With the construction of these temples in brick and later temples in stone a clear distinction developed; religious buildings were built as a long-lasting witness to the glory of their gods, whereas domestic structures—even palaces—were the dwelling places of mere mortals. Sandstone became a noble material fit only for the gods, and that is why even the royal palaces are said to have been built with timber.

The Roluos temples were built with bricks that were thinner than usual and laid in a lime mortar. The builders originally intended, it seems, to expose the brickwork in the six towerlike shrines of Preah Ko. Under the later plaster layers, a thin reddish coating appears to have served as an outer decorative surface over the brickwork. Later this original concept was elaborated by the addition of the newly discovered material sandstone, and such elements as the door surrounds and sculpted temple guardians were defined in stone. In one of the temples of Lolei the doorway was carved from one piece of stone—a surprising achievement, and a clear indication that the builders were working in a new material. Close examination of the temple towers show that the brickwork was cut out to allow the insertion of beautifully sculpted stone images flanking the doorways. At this time, it was obviously decided to plaster over the brickwork with finely worked stucco. The stone carving was of exceptional quality; many people ask themselves on seeing some of the stone lintels whether they are a recent restoration or even a piece of molded concrete. The workmanship has all the characteristics of the highest quality of carved timberwork, with deep undercutting and exquisite detailing. It is nevertheless over a thousand years old.

In a very short period, three important building materials were introduced to a country that had little experience using anything other than timber. There are brick kilns in the vicinity, and a series of potters' kilns in the neighborhood have recently come to light. It is probable that stucco was used, as it that can be modeled to simulate finely sculpted stonework. Producing stucco is a complicated procedure, requiring the slaking of lime as well as the correct proportion of grit and binders to create a material that is malleable and yet durable.

Close to Preah Ko, the temple of Bakong also dates from the end of the ninth century, the first temple in the Angkor region to represent the temple-mountain style. Here new techniques were being developed, and indeed construction took on a whole different scale. The base or platform of the temple, which represents Mount Meru, is built somewhat like a pyramid. The moat around the temple represents the oceans; the towers, the peaks; and the various levels on the pyramid, the rice terraces. The temple shrines themselves represent the five peaks.

Pre Rup, a man-made temple mountain, is the greatest temple built prior to Angkor Wat. Pre Rup was once the central feature of its own city, a city that has long since disappeared, although it is likely that the East Baray created its northern boundary. The temple mountain follows a typical design, with a fine series of diminishing terraces supporting a quincunx of shrines representing the five peaks of the mountain on the topmost terrace. Another interesting feature found in Pre Rup is a series of long galleries set close against the inner laterite wall. A feature of tenth-century architecture, these galleries were merged to form the continuous galleries found in later temples. The temple shrines are built of small, compact bricks, which were roughened so that decorative stucco could be applied. The terraced pyramid is built of a high-quality laterite, with strong horizontal architectural moldings. Of a similar style and period, the temple of East Mebon is like Pre Rup built on a laterite base, and its towers, which exhibit some of the finest

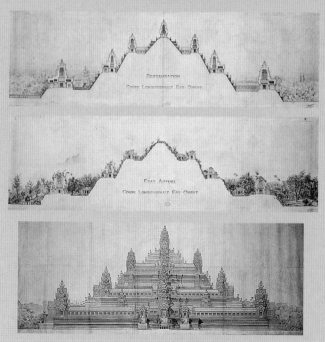

Ink and watercolor illustration and elevation drawings of Baphuon by Lucien Fournereau from an exhibition at the Paris Salon in 1890.

carved lintels, are of brick. Although nothing remains, the brickwork of these towers has been prepared for a decorative stucco finish.

Another striking temple mountain of the same period is Ta Keo, a colossal structure and the first with shrines built entirely in stone. Today, with its clean lines, the Ta Keo's simplicity reminds one of postmodern architecture, its strikingly undecorated stone blocks stacked atop one another clearly showing its structural form. This temple provides important evidence as to the process of embellishing the temples of Angkor. A close inspection makes it evident that the builder intended for it to be carved, since many of the backs or inaccessible architectural elements had been carved before they were set in place.

In strong contrast to these colossal temple mountains, and somewhat remote from Angkor proper, lies the temple of Banteay Srei, whose impact on the architectural development of the Khmer empire should not be minimized. Often referred to as the Jewel of Angkor, both for its exceptional beauty and for its size, this temple was built not by a king but by one of King Rajendravarman's counselors. Although small by comparison to all the other temples, it still retains a special grandeur and scale that is enhanced by its exquisite carvings. Built of a very fine quality pink sandstone, probably quarried locally from the Kulen Hills, the detail and depth of sculpting are unmatched elsewhere. The antefixes to the main shrines are miniature copies of the shrines they embellish, and their placement at four levels up the tower increases their splendor. The craftsmen even went to great lengths to chamfer the niches containing the delicately carved images on the main shrine, providing a false perspective. They also carved the feet of the divinities from the front, avoiding the unnatural sideways stance common to all similar divinities elsewhere.

As a precursor to Angkor Wat, there is the great temple mountain of the Baphuon. Built only fifty years after Banteay Srei, this is an extraordinary departure in size and style. In its present condition it is hard to envisage the temple as Chou Ta-kuan describes it, "a Tower of Bronze . . . a truly astonishing spectacle with more than ten chambers at its base." Although it is under major restoration, and access to the central pyramid is restricted, we can now begin to appreciate this temple complex and its new additions to the architectural style of Angkor. The Baphuon, like many of the temples within the later enclosure of Angkor Thom, has undergone several changes and additions. Like Phimeanakas, the Baphuon belonged to an earlier period, and it seems a little out of place in its present setting, squeezed between the Bayon and the first royal palace compound. It is approached along an imposing elevated causeway, which is interrupted just over halfway along by a small pavilion, which may have been the earlier outer *gopura*. The rectangular pyramid of the main temple rises beyond, in five levels, and three concentric galleries encircle the central shrine.

The central tower collapsed sometime in the sixteenth century, and with the advent of Theravada Buddhism, a colossal reclining Buddha was created along the lower western gallery, reusing stones that had fallen from the tower. The image was constructed to be carved in situ, but only the outline of the head and feet are discernible, as it was never finished. The enclosing sandstone-clad laterite walls were filled with sand to create the tapering terraces of the mountain structure, and the pressure of the weight of sand and of the central tower has caused the terraces to collapse several times. The temple was in a very ruinous state when the Ecole Française d'Extrême-Orient (EFEO), prior to the civil disturbances in the 1970s, commenced a major undertaking to restore it, one of many major restorations the EFEO undertook during the first hundred years of its commitment to working at Angkor.

The vast city of Angkor Wat, which occupies 494 acres (200 hectares), is said to have been built in thirty-seven years over an earlier temple complex, parts of which have been identified in the northeast corner of the complex. Within Angkor Wat there must also have been a royal palace, which would have been typically located on the north side of the compound. The palace, along with the dwellings of the city and the covered walkways leading down from the steps along the central causeway, would have been constructed of timber, and all evidence of these aboveground structures has long since disappeared.

To get a sense of scale and proportion, it is worth studying more closely the man-made mountain for Angkor Wat. The temple's mountain and the main shrine were formed of enclosing laterite walls, the first of which measured 1,155 by 846 feet (352 by 258 m), creating a large platform measuring more than 22 acres (9 hectares). This platform alone required 392,000 cubic yards (300,000 cu m) of fill, or 30,000 truckloads of sand, to fill it. The main pyramid, which is about 200 feet (60 m) square, rises from a second platform measuring about 300 by 430 feet (90 x 130 m) to a height of 138 feet (42 m). Each of these stages is filled with sand. The laterite acts as a retaining wall for the fill and is covered by large blocks of sandstone, which help to hold the laterite and fill in place.

In Eleanor Mannikka's essay (p. 102), we learn of the extraordinary precision with which Angkor Wat was built and its cosmological powers. At a different level, the outstanding bas-reliefs adorning the walls provide another unique dimension to this outstanding architectural masterpiece. These are undoubtedly one of the most celebrated forms of Khmer art, matching any other sculptural work of genius worldwide. In Asian circles the myths and legends they depict are well known, and every country has its own variations, but they are an inspiration to all. They tell the tales of the Ramayana and Mahabharata epics, describe the creation of the elixir of everlasting life in the Churning of the Sea of Milk, and offer insights into life at the time of the temple's construction, with the historic procession of King Suryavarman II, the temple's builder, as well as a dramatic depiction of the judgment of Yama, the god of death, mounted on a water buffalo, and scenes from heaven and hell. These great works of art extend over 1,968 feet (600 m) around the encircling arcaded galleries at the base of the temple mountain. Another interesting architectural feature is the Cruciform Gallery, located on the western approach, which leads to the upper level and the quincunx of towers that soar to the heavens, leaving the onlooker in wonderment.

Everywhere you look are carvings of awe-inspiring quality and detail. There are over 2,000 exquisitely sculpted *devata* images, each one unique; even the foliage decoration conceals figures disguised among the vegetation. Over every doorway a finely carved fronton details a vignette from one of the epics or a divinity and consorts. The workmanship defies superlatives—it is indeed the work of the gods themselves.

The Bayon is an enigma. Despite extended research, historians are still trying to piece together its chronological development. It is known that Jayavarman was the inspiration behind its simple cruciform shape. Over the years many changes were made—adding further shrines at different levels, raising the platforms, and adding more of the faced towers—creating the mystery as well as the confusion apparent today. The principal platform is square, and at the lower level a series of exposed outer galleries contains a wonderful collection of bas-reliefs depicting battles and historical events. Intermingled with the armies and armadas of boats are intriguing local scenes that help to illustrate in one's mind a picture of Angkor in its heyday: vignettes of cooking, cockfighting, wrestling, and circus scenes with jugglers, as well as wonderful interpretations of such wild animals as the rhinoceros roaming the jungles. Of course the most striking feature of the Bayon is its enigmatic faces, each a unique character that smiles down on you as you wend your way around the complex plan of the upper shrine.

In contrast the later temple or monastic complexes of Ta Prohm, Banteay Kdei, and Preah Khan emulate to some extent the temple-mountain concept, but on a linear basis. These complexes are extensive, and the ground rises a few yards on its way to the central tower, which represents Mount Meru. The enclosure walls that encircle and divide various stages within the temple complex are built to create the illusion of a flattened pyramid, surrounded by the primordial ocean represented by the moat. These Buddhist-inspired temple complexes are very different in all aspects from the temples previously constructed.

Jayavarman VII is said to have visited Lanka, an island off India's southern coast, where he was inspired by the teachings of Buddha. Jayavarman's inspiration led to the construction of four monastery temples—Banteay Kdei, Ta Prohm, Preah Khan, and Ta Som—all of a similar layout and disposition. Ta Prohm, probably the first to be built, was dedicated to the king's mother in 1186. Its main attraction today is that it was left by the EFEO in its "natural state," in the stranglehold of many magnificent ficus trees. At the time of discovery this was an inspired decision, lending it a singular atmosphere; but as with all growing things, the trees have a finite life span, which is slowly running out.

After his inspirational travels, Jayavarman decided to create more than just a temple at Preah Khan; he planned to create a large city, possibly with a temporary palace and a Buddhist center for learning. A tour of the site reveals some of Preah Khan's unique qualities.

The temple complex has been sympathetically conserved as a partial ruin, and it is well maintained and presented in a jungle setting. We can now recognize many of Jayavarman's original intentions. Many special features clearly denote Preah Khan as a royal compound. Access from the east—opened after years of clearing—gives a true perspective of Preah Khan's majestic splendor. A processional way lined on both sides by small pillars leads onto a causeway over the moat, which is edged by great *naga* motifs. Standing on the moat you see part of the 1.9-mile (3-km) enclosure wall surrounding the temple complex. Along this wall, spaced at regular intervals, are sixty-eight large sandstone *garudas* with *nagas* underfoot, which are the protectors of the compound—the *garudas* guard the heavens, while the *nagas* watch over the earth. It is often said that the *garudas*, with their arms held high, appear as a team to be supporting the whole temple in the sky. The approach through the main *gopura* follows a path that originally passed through a bustling townscape, long since disappeared, to the temple enclosure. The temple is raised on a platform, separating the raised sacred area from the profane.

A large cruciform platform extends in front of the east *gopura*. It leads along the principal axial route into the temple and to the central shrine, where a statue of the bodhisattva Lokesvara, carved in the image of Jayavarman's father, Dharanindravarman, once stood. Interesting architectural features such as the two-story pavilion, the place where the Preah Khan or sacred sword was kept, show a new building style with drum columns and, originally, a pitched tile roof. This structure, which the EFEO found as a total ruin, so intrigued scholars when they first saw it in the 1920s that it was decided thirty years later to rebuild it as we see it today, using a system developed in Java and known as anastylosis. The Hall of Dancers is another spectacular architectural masterpiece, with its large open nave leading to unusual little open courtyards off the main cruciform space. The openings to these are spanned by large lintels decorated with sublime dancing *apsaras* imbued with *soma*, the elixir of everlasting life.

Four enclosure walls ring the Preah Khan compound—one more than usual. Following the great battle where Jayavarman VII finally defeated the Chams, he decided to honor his generals by dedicating small shrines to them within the Buddhist sanctum sanctorum. It was necessary therefore to enlarge the sanctum by enclosing it with a circumambulatory wall providing access to these shrines.

In recognition of Hinduism, which was still the official state religion, Jayavarman dedicated a series of peripheral shrines to Hindu divinities—Vishnu to the west, Shiva to the north, and the practice of ancestor worship to the south. The east served as the grandiose approach to the central shrine.

It is interesting that, prior to the construction of his palace complex in Angkor Thom, Jayavarman VII is believed to have built a temporary palace in Preah Khan. Recent archaeological explorations here have identified an archaeological site in the northeast sector of the 138-acre (56-hectare) compound, where there is evidence of a moated island with a large central tank. The tank is surrounded by raised ground; more than likely a timber structure would have here served as a temporary palace while Jayavarman built his new palace in Angkor Thom alongside his state temple, Bayon.

Religious practices in Hindu temples are complex, but their space requirement is minimal. Although these shrines are lofty and highly decorated, they have a very small sanctum, offering just enough room for the deity and a few priests. However, the temple complexes are vast in scale, because they house hundreds of divinities. When Preah Khan was constructed, an inscription provided instructions as to how the divinities should be worshiped and in what order. At least 300 divinities were housed in the temple complex, the inscription tells us. Most of the temples were laid out following a typical theme, enclosed by a boundary wall and accessible through an ornate *gopura* or gateway from the east. It appears that in Hindu temples dedicated to Shiva the principal entrances were from the east. The main exception to this rule is at Angkor Wat, which was dedicated to Vishnu and where the principal entrance is decidedly from the west. The east entrance is very plain and simple by comparison.

The layout of the temples and palaces and their attributes quickly make clear their relative importance. At royal compounds such as the Angkor Thom complex, Angkor Wat, and Preah Khan, a moat enclosed the whole complex, whereas at most other temples, as in Ta Prohm and Banteay Srei, the moats surrounded just the temple complex itself. The palace compounds thus made a very grand architectural statement, with their great *naga* balusters lining either side of the causeway over the moats, which led to magnificent *gopuras*. The causeways are often described as rainbows from Earth to heaven, and the moats as great oceans.

Few religious buildings in the world match the scale and proportions of the great temples of Angkor. However, it seems that the builders wanted to create even more of an illusion of grandeur by using skillful trompe l'oeils to further aggrandize the structures. In the days when the temples were used for religious festivals, the religious areas would never have been as crowded as they are today, yet there was still this desire to intimidate the worshiper and exalt the gods. The temple and shrine were like a large theater set, in which corridors would come to a dead end; doorways and windows would be carved onto the wall surface to maintain symmetry, and thousands of sculpted images would decorate the facades.

The most obvious way of creating grandeur was to make the stairways steep and exaggerate the height of the risers. A more subtle device, however, was narrowing the stairway at the top, creating a sense of false perspective. Many such examples exist in Angkor Wat, Ta Keo, and Phimeanakas. The perspectives are so subtle that the average person will believe the illusion is real!

An interesting comparison can be made to religious structures being built in Europe at the same time. At the height of the Angkor building period, during the reign of Jayavarman VII, monuments such as Notre Dame in Paris were being constructed. This church demonstrated the great engineering feat of the true vault, which could span large distances. Similarly, in England many great cathedrals, such as Durham Cathedral, with its soaring columns and filigree vaulting, were spanning large naves. The difference in scale and construction time was very marked—these great monuments to Christianity took centuries to build and were often a compendium of differing architectural styles, whereas the temples of Angkor were built within the lifetime of their sponsors.

BUILDING MATERIALS

Before the arrival of the great Khmer empire, life would have been very simple and straightforward. Domestic structures would have been simple stilted houses, and even the small shrines would have been built of timber. It was therefore a major transition to move in a few decades from this simple form of construction to the ever more complex temple structures, using permanent materials such as brick and stone.

Brickwork was the first durable material to be used in the construction of the temples. Early temples such as Preah Ko and Lolei, in the Roluos group, were built of brick, as was the early-tenth-century temple Prasat Kravan. However, by the end of the tenth century, bricks were no longer used in construction.

Brick

Undoubtedly the concept of building in bricks came from India, and it is interesting to speculate how difficult it would have been for Khmer builders to find appropriate clay, as the soil close to Angkor is mostly sandy. Another problem was to find sufficient lime to make mortar and stucco, as no limestone deposits exist in the neighborhood. Mollusk shells obtained from the nearby rivers or from the Tonle Sap, burned, supplied lime, and clay deposits were to be found locally in Dam Deik and also in Ta Nei, where recently a pottery kiln has been unearthed by an archaeological team from Sophia University, Tokyo. The bricks used by the Khmers are small and very dense. The joints, filled with a lime putty, are also surprisingly tight, a quality achieved by forming a hollow in the brick during manufacture and by rubbing the bricks together when laying them. The bricks are dark red, with slight variations according to their proximity to the heat during the firing process.

Stucco

It is thought that some of the temples were left with exposed brickwork for a short time and, as with the temples in Roluos, later stuccoed. Based on remnants found on some temples, the quality of stucco produced in the tenth century matches that of the superb sculpted stone lintels that were part of the overall design. The stucco was made using slaked lime, sand of varying grain sizes, and an additive such as palm sugar. Before applying the stucco, the brickwork or apparently even the stonework would be prepared—details would be carved into the backing material, or it would be hacked to provide a gripping surface for the stucco—prior to the application of at least three coats of plaster. Each coat would be more refined in both detail and finish, providing a solid and waterproof coating as well as a highly ornate finish. All the surviving details to be seen today belong to the early temples. However, traces of stucco on some later twelfth-century temples, such as the central shrines of Ta Som and Preah Khan, give credence to the present-day speculation that the facades were embellished with elaborate rococolike ornamentation.

Sandstone

The great quantities of sandstone used to build these vast monuments were by no means close at hand. The quarries were located in the Kulen Hills, approximately 30 miles (50 km) to the northeast of Angkor. The full extent of the quarries is not yet definitively known. The Kulen Hills were a Khmer Rouge stronghold, and mines and ordnance are still being cleared from this area. It is generally thought that there were quarries providing building stone along the length of the Kulen Hills, but the best example of a working quarry is located at the eastern end of this sandstone outcrop.

A visit to a quarry at the eastern end of the Kulen Hills, recently reopened to provide stone for restoration in Angkor, provides a telling insight into the method of quarrying. In the Kulen quarries the stone was open mined, a process that differs from the typical image of a stone quarry, where stone is cut from a cliff face. We were told that the quarry, close to the temple of Beng Mealea, extends over a five-mile (8 km) stretch along the base of the hills, which rise steeply from this plain. The original scars of quarrying were evident by large indentations in the ground, and we knew we were walking over what had formerly been the quarry bed for the stones of Angkor. In the searing heat, with not a breath of wind to cool their sweating bodies, a gang of quarrymen were cutting stone, using eight-foot (2.5 m) crowbars three inches (8 cm) in diameter, with sharpened ends. A line was drawn on the quarry bed, and with these giant chisels, large pieces of stone measuring a minimum of thirteen to sixteen feet (4–5 m) in length and about 3 feet (1 m) square in section were cut by hand and split from the stone bed. The only noise audible above the screeching cicadas was the *thunk-thunk* of metal hitting stone as the workers chiseled three-inch (8 cm) cuts along the line into the stone bed to a depth of about three feet (1 m). Using the principle of leverage in the form of long poles cut from tree trunks and a few well-placed horizontal incisions, workers pried the stones from their bed and rolled them over, ready for transportation. It can take a team of five men as long as five days to cut one stone, which will be shaped to form a square monolithic pillar in Angkor Wat or one of Jayavarman VII's temples.

Cutting the stone is simple in comparison to getting it to the building site. Today it is still a struggle to load these massive stones weighing in excess of eleven tons (10 t) onto a large diesel truck, which has to find its way to Angkor along potholed tracks through the jungle. As was the case at many other major sites of this period, little is known about the original methods of transporting these stones to the temple sites.

One fanciful means of transportation was illustrated in Henri Mouhot's book; a sculpture floats on a bamboo raft along a river or canal. Stories abounded about stones being floated on large bamboo rafts along the Siem Reap River, formerly a canal, whose source rises in the Kulen Hills. A recent piece of practical research carried out in the Preah Khan moat soon put an end to this speculation; the raft could barely carry the weight of a human, let alone an eleven-ton stone! If stones were to be floated, we calculated that 1,000 pieces of bamboos would be necessary to provide sufficient buoyancy. A more likely system would have been to roll the stones along the very sophisticated road systems using elephants. Another possibility is that, once the stones had reached the edge of the Tonle Sap, larger boats might have been used to float them to their destination.

On any site, evidence abounds on how the stones were moved around and worked. A small bas-relief in the Bayon, located in an interior gallery south of the western access to the upper level, depicts the system of maneuvering the stones using ropes. It illustrates how stones are lifted and answers a frequently asked question: Why are many pairs of holes cut into the stone? These pairs of holes were probably cut using chisels in the quarries themselves and it is thought that the stones may have been partially prepared or "dressed" at the same time. Bamboo pegs were rammed into the holes and wetted, causing them to swell and grip the stone. Ropes or even vines were then interwoven between the pegs and when lifting took place, a sideways pressure was applied to the pegs, giving added friction. The bas-relief also illustrates the principles of the block and tackle for lifting the stones. The use of fixed pulleys seemed common practice in the quarries, but it is interesting to see that the principle of mechanical advantage—the use of two pulley blocks, a fixed pulley and a moving pulley, which reduces the load but requires the rope to be pulled twice the distance—enabling large stones to be lifted was also understood.

The Bayon bas-relief also illustrates a system of polishing the stone's surface to achieve extraordinarily tight joints between stones. Two stones that were to be laid adjacent to one another would be prepared by rubbing the two blocks together, with abrasive sand placed between them. The upper stone, suspended from scaffolding using ropes and pegs, slid over the lower one. Experiments to see if this system works have been carried out recently, raising some doubt as to its effectiveness, especially regarding the time it takes to produce anything approaching a smooth surface.

A close examination of the many temple facades makes it evident that the structures were built in blocks brought direct from the quarry and stacked in a hitherto incomprehensible system or methodology to create walls. Although their skills in masonry seem to have been lacking, the craftsmen developed various carpentry techniques to construct, for example, doorways with great ingenuity.

From a practical point of view it is fairly obvious that a series of different areas were quarried. The color, quality, and strength of the stone provide clues as to its original location. Many of the temples built by Jayavarman VII used a greenish gray stone that proved easier to cut and was of very good quality and long lasting. Typical examples of this type of stone are to be found in the Bayon and Preah Khan. A yellowish gray stone is very inferior in strength and quality, and probably its bed was located fairly close to the general surrounding ground level. It is certainly the least well formed sandstone, its failings due to the presence of clay between the horizontal laminations of sand. The third type of sandstone is the exquisite pink sandstone from which Banteay Srei, the jewel of Angkor, is built. In striking contrast to those mentioned previously, this is a very special and evenly colored pink sandstone, which is also extremely durable. Most of the structures built with this stone have been through severe monsoon conditions as well as being totally eclipsed by the jungle, and their sculptured surfaces have survived intact.

Laterite

The other important building stone used in Angkor is laterite, a yellow volcanic sedimentary rock with a complex chemical content, mixed with clay. In Angkor it was used to help create the massive pyramidal platforms for the temples and to construct the long enclosure walls, saving the sandstone for the more decorative facing work. Laterite is very local; in fact Angkor is built on a natural bed of laterite, and it is conjectured that during the excavation of the moats encircling many of the temples, the laterite was quarried and used to construct hidden structures. It is still uncertain whether laterite, when used to construct walls, was intended to be exposed or whether it was plastered. In several instances it was used in place of sandstone, most probably because the sandstone had been used up and there was no time to get a further supply from the quarry. Such examples of substitution can be seen in Ta Som, a temple that we know to have been built in a hurry and not considered an important shrine. Preah Khan contains several examples of later structures built in laterite—the circumambulatory cloister between enclosure walls I and II, for example, or the large platform opposite the two-story pavilion.

Metals

Metals must have existed, as they were used in the Khmer empire. There was probably an iron source in the Kulen Hills. Later, iron was smelted from laterite, a material found somewhere close to Preah Khan and Kompong Svay. Iron staples and butterfly clamps have been found at many sites, indicating that iron was used to some extent to consolidate the stone structures. A very visible example of this can be seen in the stone "paneling" applied to the terraces of the Bakong. At each corner where the stone panels abut, a hole shows where originally a metal clamp fixed the stones. The holes were made to remove the iron, which was reused in weapons. Chou Ta-kuan's *Customs of Cambodia* makes several references to towers covered in bronze or gold—the Baphuon, the Bayon, and Phimeanakas. Possibly these towers were sheathed in metal sheets and gilded. Preah Khan's inscription refers to large quantities of bronze sheets. It is speculated that these sheets were fixed to timber frames, which had been nailed to the walls of the central tower and its anteroom. The rust from these nails can still be seen in Preah Khan.

Construction Methods

Ideally sandstone should be cut from its quarry bed and reset in a structure as it is taken from the quarry. However, the tendency at the time of construction was to reset the stone with the original laminations running vertically, a common way of forming columns. The columns were under compression, but with the laminations running vertically the stone column is at its weakest. There are many instances where columns have split their full length. Another common failure is at the base of the column because the stone lamination is exposed and will draw water in by capillary action. When moisture encounters these clays, which normally expand when moistened, the column bases start to delaminate and lose their bearing strength. Similar problems exist where salts exist between the laminations; the salts expand when they dry out and, trapped in the laminates, cause a similar process of delamination. Angkor Wat has been built using this inferior-quality sandstone, and especially on the exposed central shrine, much of the detail is fast disappearing.

Normally building in stone follows the principle of post-and-lintel construction. A set of vertical blocks of stone—the posts—carries a horizontal stone, the lintel. As stone is a compressive rather than a tensile material, it is best used to carry vertical loads through its mass. When used as a lintel, the stone is subjected to tensile stress, and as it has very little elasticity, if overloaded it tends to fail or fracture. The system of corbeling was developed to span larger openings, as in this form of construction loading is transferred from one stone to another vertically and in compression. Apparently the Khmers had no tradition for working stone, and their lack of understanding in the use of this material is all too evident, especially in some early stone structures.

The foundations of most of the temples are very simple. Where excavations have exposed the footings of a structure, the structure may reach a depth of less than three feet (1 m) below ground level. Often the foundations are simply an extension of the structure above, and it appears that the ground has been cleared and leveled, with little other preparation. However, two natural phenomena may account for this lack of foundations deep enough to match the size of the structures they support. First, the soil is predominantly sandy, which provides an excellent overall distribution of the structural loading; and second, a natural bed of laterite rests a few yards on average belowground under most of the principle temples.

The walls therefore rise directly from the ground, usually with a molding, following the plan so often seen in classical buildings. After they were quarried and brought to site, the stones were laid in a very random fashion, often without the courses, or layers, of stone blocks on the same level. The blocks were laid dry, with no mortar in the joints, and these joints are so tight—it is impossible to get a dollar bill between the stones. Once in place, the stones were dressed and carved in situ as previously described.

In a number of earlier stone temples, such as the Baphuon, many of the methods of construction and jointing of the stones bear standard timber-working details. For example, door frames are often made using mortice and tenon joints exactly as a timber frame would have been built. Several temples have odd details such as horizontal supports to columns, which would provide stiffness in a timber structure but is ineffectual with stone, where the column is carrying a heavy load in compression. This detail in fact has caused many failures in the temples; mortice and tenon joints cut into the columns cause an inherent weakness, diminishing their compressive strength.

The question of stone color raises another interesting debate. Were these massive structures meant to be seen as masterpieces built in stone, or was the stone a base material that would then be plastered over? We will return to this theory later, but I use it to illustrate the importance of the stone's color. There are three basic colors or hues—common grayish green, yellowish gray, and pink sandstone. The most striking examples of these different colors are to be seen in the temples of Ta Keo, Angkor Wat, and Banteay Srei. The stone's color is also an indication as to its quality. For example, the grayish green sandstone in Ta Keo, the only temple not to have been profusely carved at the time of construction, is said to have come from a layer of stone in the quarry known as the "King's Bed," a stone bed of exceptional hardness.

It is often questioned why the temple was never finished. During a visit to Ta Keo, which literally translates as "Temple of Crystal," with a stonemason we debated this point. Close inspection of the towers provides evidence of an intention to carve the facade on completion of the construction phase, as many of the backs of the octagonal pilasters that support the decorated lintels over doorways were precarved before placement. The stonemason put forward a theory that the stone from the King's Bed was too hard to carve, quickly blunting the mason's chisels. Other theories are that the royal patron, King Jayavarman v, died before the temple was completed, or that the temple was struck by lightning, which in Hindu belief is an inauspicious sign. Nevertheless, Ta Keo remains to this day a valuable example of construction of the Angkor temples.

The process of carving in situ is also an unusual feature at Angkor. Take for example the great bas-reliefs at Angkor Wat and Bayon. These masterpieces were all carved in a vertical position, rather as a mural is painted. Many hundreds of masons probably worked on each stretch of wall under the guidance of a master mason, who would have drawn cartoons as a guide to the overall design. In several places on the bas-reliefs of the Bayon the process can be clearly seen. The outlines of the picture have been engraved into the stone and left incomplete. Similarly, many *devatas* and *asuras* on the Terrace of the Leper King still bear the chisel marks of incomplete work.

One early exception to the vaulted space can be seen in the Bakong complex. The small vestibules leading onto the platform proper, which like the platform are built of sandstone, have what can best be described as pitched or sloping roofs. The roofs were made of stone, which spanned the full length of the pitch, and these sizable stone slabs interlocked with one another. This showed great ingenuity but a total lack of understanding of the qualities of sandstone. The roofs were propped up by the EFEO using reinforced concrete, and the concrete has failed and is in turn supported with large beams of timber!

Another method for roof construction was to use timber rafters with a roof covering of clay tiles. This system follows that used for domestic and palace structures, and an example of a standing structure that was roofed in this way can be seen in the two-story pavilion in Preah Khan.

As the principles for construction were limited to either corbeled brickwork or stonework, there were no large vaulted spaces. In fact the largest span in Angkor is said to be that of the nave in the Hall of Dancers, which formerly spanned a distance of about twenty feet (6 m). The stability of a corbeled or crude vault depends entirely on gravity or vertical dead weight. The method of constructing a corbeled vault in stone is very simple: slabs of stone are set one above the other, projecting one-third their total length beyond the stone below. This process is continued from both walls until the stones meet, forming a crude arch. The meeting stones are capped by a ridge stone, which is often decorated by finials. In a corbeled vault, unlike a true vault, there is no horizontal thrust. In Angkor the sizes of stone measure about 5 feet (1.5 m) in length, 2.5 feet (75 cm) in width, and 1.6 feet (50 cm) in height. However, these stone units are skillfully contrived to overlap with the adjacent stones, and an elaborate series of weep holes allows rainwater to flow from the peak of the roof to its lower edge. There are of course limits to the spans that can be formed, and this distance has in many cases dictated the module for the construction of many temples. The arch was never introduced into any Angkorian structures. Brick vaults are made of much smaller units, of course, but the principle of construction is the same.

BUILDING INTERIORS AND DECORATION

Today's visitors are very aware of the high thresholds that need to be crossed to enter every structure. These consist of massive stones, sometimes with small steps on either side—"moonstones," cut in the shape of a lotus—which aid the visitor over the threshold. Today we can admire the accuracy with which these structures were set out as we cast our eyes down miles of corridor or up gigantic flights of stairs, marveling at the precision with which the structures are aligned. It is important to remember, however, that on each of the thresholds along these grand vistas we see today, a pair of timber doors would be opened and closed as the procession of royalty or priests passed from one shrine to the other. If you look carefully, you can see the sockets into which the lintels supporting the upper door pintel would have been inserted, and the socket in which the bottom pintels would have turned. Another strong architectural feature missing today is the wood-coffered ceilings, which would have concealed the crude stone vaults and towers. These ceilings, which like all the ephemeral materials of the time have long ago disintegrated, were built at cornice level and would have completely changed the proportions and scale of the temple compounds. In contrast to the way they look today, the temples would have been dark, with perhaps only small oil lamps to light the shrines.

One of the great debates among the historians of Angkor and the Khmer is whether or not the temples were highly decorated, as classical Greek temples in fact were, hiding all the fine stone detailing that is so admired today. There has been extensive speculation concerning the decoration in Angkor, especially of the great sandstone structures. We are usually in awe of the stone structures, admiring the beauty of their sculpted surfaces. However, if we take a closer look at both the exterior and interior wall surfaces in most temples, we will find remnants of white plaster. More evidence exists in the interiors, as they were better protected, and in the last few years this speculation has been verified to some extent in one of the secondary shrines at Preah Ko and in the central shrine of the western Vishnu complex in Preah Khan, where traces of decorative wall paintings have been discovered.

The early brick temples were decorated with extremely fine stucco work. Due to the humid climate, the likelihood of finding remnants or any external wall paintings is remote. Fortunately, Chou Ta-kuan gives us very colorful descriptions of both the Khmers of the thirteenth century and their buildings. His account of the bronze and golden towers and lead-covered roofs has encouraged further field research, strengthening the case for the colorful decoration of the temples. In the field, when studying Preah Khan's central tower, one immediately notices how basic and undecorated this most significant of all the temple's shrines is. On closer scrutiny, large pieces of stucco are visible in protected corners, and one immediately recalls the highly sophisticated plaster decoration found on the earlier temples. It is possible to apply gilding to stuccowork, and thus the central tower of Preah Khan could indeed have been golden. In the antechamber to the central shrine as well as the central shrine itself, the wall surface is pockmarked with uniform holes. These holes did not serve to facilitate the moving of the stones but probably supported a timber frame onto which bronze sheets were fixed. We might also speculate that these sheets were also etched and gilded. Closer inspection of several temples will reveal similar indicators to their being highly ornate and colorful.

THE REDISCOVERY OF ANGKOR AND RECENT CONSERVATION EFFORTS

The rediscovery of Angkor is often dated around the 1860s, when the celebrated French explorer Henri Mouhot stumbled upon it during his botanical travels in Siam, Cambodia, and Laos. Later research reveals that Mouhot was not the first to discover Angkor, however, nor did he claim to be. He nevertheless created a general awareness of Angkor and provided Europe with pictures of this remarkable site. In fact Angkor was never totally lost, as we have started to learn following more recent research. It seems that the Portuguese Dominicans were some of the first explorers to journey to Angkor in the middle sixteenth century, about a century after its recorded period of abandonment. Later there is evidence that the Spanish were in Angkor at the end of the sixteenth century, and there are texts also proposing that Angkor was built by Alexander the Great or the Romans. A group of Japanese merchants visited the site in the seventeenth century, and their party prepared a detailed plan of Angkor Wat.

Cambodia was colonized by the French in 1864, along with Vietnam and Laos, into a single protectorate known as Indochina. At about this time the Ecole Française d'Extrême-Orient (EFEO) was established as an academic research center, and a period of intense study began in Angkor. During this time the EFEO developed a remarkable archive of survey drawings and archaeological notes, and also carried out extensive restoration and anastylosis of many major sites in Angkor.

The Angkor Conservancy was the local administrative arm of the Cambodian government, which was set up in collaboration with the EFEO in 1901. Soon after, with the EFEO's help, it took charge of Angkor. It was around this time that the first systematic inventory of the monuments of Angkor was drawn up by Etienne Lunet de Lajonquière. The project took him and his team about seven years to complete, and during this time Lajonquière prepared some stunningly beautiful architectural drawings of the monuments of Angkor. These drawings, lost for almost a century, were only recently rediscovered in a roll in an attic above the old EFEO offices in Paris. Jean Commaille was the first French conservator to be appointed with the responsibility of administering the historic site of Angkor. Sadly, his time in Angkor was short-lived; he was assassinated by bandits when they stole the meager wages he was carrying to pay his workforce. Henri Marchal, who worked tirelessly and with fervor to clear and restore the monuments of Angkor, soon replaced Commaille. In 1930 Marchal went to Java to study the system known as anastylosis being developed by the Dutch for the reconstruction of historic monuments. In this method, structures are carefully dismantled after being documented, then rebuilt exactly in their original form, using matching materials and construction methods. Marchal was later to return to Angkor and test anastylosis for the first time in Banteay Srei between 1931 and 1936. In 1923 Banteay Srei had been discovered as a total ruin by none other than André Malraux, later to be the French minister of culture. At this time he had in fact looted the site, making off with several beautiful *devatas (srei)*. Malraux was caught when the boatload of booty arrived in Phnom Penh, and put under house arrest for his misdeeds. His case nevertheless brought the site to prominence. Shortly after its discovery, Henri Marchal reconstructed this unique little masterpiece with great skill and perseverance, establishing a methodology that would be used on several of the other temples that came under the EFEO's purview.

Marchal continued to live in Cambodia until 1947, when he died at the great age of eighty-seven. He was replaced as chief conservator by Georges Trouvé, a brilliant figure in the field of archaeology. Perhaps one of Trouvé's greatest finds was the Buddha in the central shrine of the Bayon. This image had been broken into pieces and buried in a pit there at a depth of several yards during Jayavarman VIII's reign. Trouvé excavated the central shrine in 1931 and finally provided proof that the Bayon was originally a Buddhist temple. The Buddha was later installed in a small sanctuary on the west side of the road leading to the Victory Gate, where it can still be found today. Trouvé also met an untimely death; his memorial can be found off the road that encircles the Bayon on the eastern side. He was followed by another distinguished conservator, Maurice Glaize, who took up his post in 1937. Glaize was responsible for some remarkable restorations, using the system of anastylosis to dismantle and reconstruct the central tower of Neak Pean, rebuilding from a pile of rubble the central tower of Bakong in Roluos, and completely restoring Banteay Samre, a little-known temple of great charm just beyond the village of Pradak on the eastern banks of the East Baray. One of Glaize's greatest contribution to Angkor, however, was its first detailed guidebook, entitled *Les Monuments du groupe Angkor* (Guide to the Angkor Monuments), and first published in 1944.

The next incumbent was Jean Laur, who spent four years as the chief conservator before handing the title over to Bernard-Philippe Groslier in 1959. Laur, along with René Dumont and Jacques Dumarcay, initiated the major restoration program at the Baphuon that is still under way today. Philippe Groslier, the son of Georges Groslier, who was well known as the creator of the National

Museum in Phnom Penh, also contributed enormously to the safeguarding of Angkor. With Jacques Dumarcay's support, Groslier continued the major works at the Baphuon and in Preah Khan and continued using the system of anastylosis in the temple of Thommanon, a stone structure at the east entrance to Angkor Thom, and in the smaller brick temple known as Prasat Kravan.

The EFEO was forced to leave Angkor due to the civil war in 1972, but has since returned to continue its invaluable research in Cambodia, celebrating a century of work at Angkor in February 2001. The work of the EFEO has provided a sound basis for the many different countries now involved in projects in Angkor. EFEO is working again in Angkor Thom on two sites — the famous eleventh-century Baphuon Temple, and the Terrace of Elephants, where a fine repair program was recently completed. Their main focus however, is still on researching and recording the many lesser-known sites on the periphery of Angkor.

In 1986, following the strife of the civil war and in a statement of nonalignment supported by Prime Minister Indira Gandhi, a team from the Archaeological Survey of India (ASI) began working at Angkor Wat. They continued for six years, cleaning and repairing many aspects of the temple. Many conservators at the time considered some of the work undertaken by the ASI insensitive and inappropriate. It should be remembered, however, that the threat of civil war was then still hanging over Kampuchea, and supplies of labor and materials were very limited.

The next group to appear on the scene was the World Monuments Fund (WMF). In December 1989 a team of specialists, invited to evaluate the damage at Angkor after twenty years of civil strife and isolation, was surprised that the temples had been relatively unaffected by the upheavals that had shaken Cambodia. Angkor's caretakers had not, however, been so fortunate; most of those with any skills in conservation had died in the killing fields. Aware of the distress caused by the lack of skilled personnel, WMF decided to put its efforts into training both professionals and craftsmen in conserving and protecting their heritage, and to help reestablish their skills, confidence, and dignity. The Preah Khan Conservation Project was set up in 1992, and a team of students and craftsmen were put to work under the guidance of a group of international conservation specialists. WMF has since developed a broad-spectrum project for this extensive 150-acre Buddhist monastic complex, which is now in ruins. The scope of work consists of conservation, repair maintenance, and presentation of the complex as a partial ruin. Nine years later, WMF is proud to support three more conservation projects at Ta Som, Angkor Wat, and a group of remote sites on the periphery of Angkor, all of which are now being run by the Khmer staff trained at Preah Khan.

Tokyo's Sophia University, which has been working in Southeast Asia for over two decades, is involved with a similar Buddhist temple complex of the same period as Preah Khan, known as Banteay Kdei, and is still actively working in Angkor today. At Banteay Kdei one of the greatest archaeological finds was made quite by chance at the beginning of 2001. During a routine excavation to establish the temple's axis, the Japanese archaeologists broke into a burial ground for sculptures. It is believed that during the reign of Jayavarman VIII, when Hindu iconoclasm swept through Angkor, removing all vestiges of Buddhism, these Buddhist sculptures were collected — 174 of them — and thrown into this pit to rid the temple of Buddhism. This discovery provides a new dimension on the history of Angkor during this uncertain period and gives Angkor perhaps a complete set of Buddhist statuary. The Sophia team has also been excavating an interesting archaeological site, Ta Nei, which was an early pottery site.

The mid-1990s saw the commencement of a series of Japanese government (JICA) supported programs. JICA has concentrated on two individual structures classified as libraries, one in the Bayon temple and the other in Angkor Wat. For several years the Japanese team has also been undertaking detailed archaeological excavations of a group of twelve tower monuments known as the Suor Prat, in the Royal Square of Angkor Thom. The team has produced an extensive archive of all its findings, providing general information relating to geology, water levels, and an archaeological database that is relevant to many other sites in Angkor.

A German team from the Fachhochschule in Cologne—the German Apsara Conservation Project—has been working since 1996 on a very interesting research and emergency intervention program to save the decorative elements of Angkor Wat, among them the famous *apsaras*, or celestial nymphs who have partaken of the elixir of everlasting life. The team's research is helping to develop and train a group of Khmer craftsmen in the process of protecting and conserving the sculptural art in Angkor Wat and to analyze the defects causing decay to the sandstone.

A team from the Indonesian government, famous for its techniques of anastylosis, has been working on the *gopuras* or gateways of the original palace compound within Angkor Thom. They successfully completed three *gopuras* and trained two archaeologists in the process of anastylosis before having to retrench due to the political situation in their country.

The Italian government, via the International Center for Conservation in Rome (ICCROM) has fielded a team to work on the tenth-century Pre Rup temple, which focused mostly on consolidating a dangerous tower structure on the lower-level east side. This team brought to Angkor a system of consolidation, wrapping the structure with high-tensile wires to prevent it from collapsing.

The most recent team to come to Angkor in 2000 is from the Republic of China's Cultural Relics Bureau. This team is working at Chau Say Tevoda, one of a pair of eleventh-century temples that flank the approach to the east *gopura* of Angkor Thom. The Chinese team has concentrated on extensive aboveground archaeology; following the pattern of several other groups, it is concentrating on the reconstruction of one of the small libraries and the raised pathway leading to the adjacent bank of the Siem Reap River.

The government has appointed APSARA (Authorité pour la Protection du Site et l'Aménagement de la Région d'Angkor)—to be the local authority controlling the activities in Angkor. The coordination of these various teams is through the International Coordinating Committee for Safeguarding Angkor (ICC), which is cochaired by the French and Japanese ambassadors to Cambodia. The United Nations Educational, Scientific and Cultural Organization (UNESCO) acts as secretariat and interlocutor between APSARA, the royal government of Cambodia, and the various teams. The ICC, which meets twice a year, monitors applications, along with APSARA, from countries and organizations interested in assisting the royal Cambodian government in safeguarding Angkor. As APSARA builds up its capabilities and professional staff, it will become wholly responsible for the caretaking of Angkor.

THE
OUTLYING
TEMPLES

N

Tonlé Sap

Phnom Krapeang

Chuor Phnom Kravanh
(Cardamom Mountains)

Phnom Sam Koh   Phnom Aoral

Phnom Knang Trapeang

Chuor Phnom Damrei
(Elephant Mountains)

GULF
OF
HAILAND

Kirirom
National Park

GULF
OF
KOMPONG
SOM   Bokor
National Park

Mekong River

BANTEAY
SAMRE

*Banteay Samre, constructed
in the mid-twelfth century by Suryavarman II,
bears a distinct resemblance to
his other great architectural achievements
of Phnom Rung, Angkor Wat,
and Beng Mealea.
Although on a smaller scale,
it is finely proportioned with superb details.
Restored by Maurice Glaize in the 1930s,
it is one of the most complete monuments
left by the Khmer.*

Top: The wide second enclosure may have contained a moat.
The tapering shape of the redented sanctuary tower, its top shaped
like a lotus bud, can be seen above the high galleries,
which were blind on this side.

Above: Rows of square sandstone pillars supported the roof
of a portico, which was open to the courtyard. Although the sanctuary
was oriented to the east, the main entrance
was from the west because of its proximity to the East Baray.

*Top: While most of Banteay Samre's bas-reliefs concern Vishnu,
scholars believe the temple may have been Buddhist.
A pediment of the north library depicts the birth of Brahma.*

*Above: The inner enclosure is compact, bounded by very high,
wide laterite galleries with balustered windows.
The raised axial terrace with exceptional* naga *balustrades
is so high that it forms four basins. The* gopuras *of
the first enclosure have three receding frontons, and gables
ending in* hooded *nagas.*

ROLUOS:

BAKONG

In the ninth century,
construction of the temples at Roluos
launched classical Khmer architecture with
several fundamental innovations,
including concentric enclosures with
gopuras, naga balustrades,
the first libraries, and narrative bas-relief.

Top: *Four levels with steep axial stairways ascend to
a high summit platform. Statues of Javanese-style seated lions
line the stairways, and twelve small prasat towers sit
on the fourth level.*

Above: *The whole temple was sheathed in sandstone, with friezes
carved around the walls of the top level, of which only
a few examples remain. This bas-relief shows asuras in battle.*

Opposite: *Indravarman I established a royal city, Hariharalaya,
near the Tonle Sap Lake and built the temple mountain
of Bakong. Doorways received elaborate decoration, and the
lintels are some of the finest in Khmer art. The temple,
found in complete ruin, was reconstructed by
Maurice Glaize in the late 1930s.*

Above: Protecting the entrance of a prasat *is the
carving of a mythical monster, a* makara,
*with garlands of foliage coming from its mouth.
A man with a sword was often depicted mounting the creature.
The design originated in Java, where
the large head of another demonic creature, the* kala,
was also used to frighten away evil spirits.

Opposite: Eight brick prasat *towers encircle the base,
two on each side. Traces of ornamental stucco
remain on the brick facades, and niches hold standing deities,
male in the eastern shrines and female in the western.*

ROLUOS:

PREAH KO

Befitting the devaraja *concept, the six brick towers of Preah Ko were dedicated in 879 to the worship of not only Shiva and Gauri, but the ancestors of the king.*

Below: Vishnu was the figure most commonly depicted in statues of the period, sculpted with four arms holding his attributes.

*Top: Three east towers pay tribute to Indravarman's paternal ancestors,
and the three smaller west towers honor his maternal forebears.*

Above: A god rides upon a kala, *or* rahu, *who holds a spray of foliage in his mouth,
from which horsemen arise. Beneath, sword-wielding deities
sit on three-headed* nagas *which are extensions of the bouquet of leaf scrolls.*

Opposite: Dvarapalas *in niches honor paternal ancestors.
The brick walls show remnants of the original overlay of stucco floral decoration.*

ROLUOS:

LOLEI

*Indravarman I created the first reservoir
used for irrigation, the Indratataka,
revolutionizing Khmer hydrology.
His son, Yasovarman I, situated an island
in the center of the baray in 893
and erected Lolei upon it.
As at Bakong, a single monolithic block
of sandstone was cut to form
each doorway.*

The west towers honor maternal ancestors and have female deities in niches.
These young monks live on the temple grounds in an active
Theravada Buddhist monastery.

Opposite: Dvarapalas holding tridents grace the east sanctuary
honoring Shiva and Yasovarman's paternal ancestors.

PHNOM
KROM

*On a hill above the north end of
the Tonle Sap Lake stands
the weathered shrine of Phnom Krom,
one of the three summit temples
built by Yasovarman I
at the end of the ninth century.
Three towers are raised on a laterite
and sandstone platform,
symbolizing Brahma, Vishnu,
and in the center, Shiva.*

TONLE
SAP LAKE
AND
FLOATING
VILLAGE

*Tonle Sap Lake is one of the
most productive freshwater fisheries
in the world. The rising and
falling waters of the largest lake
in southeast Asia protect
flooded forests and provide a
breeding ground for fish and birds.
The fishing villages on stilts and
the style of fish traps and nets remain
the same as those illustrated
in the bas-reliefs of Bayon.*

BANTEAY
SREI

*Twenty-one miles (25 km) northeast of Angkor,
in a dense forest near the Kulen Hills,
is the miniature shrine of Banteay Srei,
considered by some as the pinnacle
of Angkor art.*

*Below: One of the best-known
sculptures from the tenth century, of
Shiva and Uma, was found
in Banteay Srei's central sanctuary.*

Top: Two libraries stand to the north and south
of the sanctuary platform. The north library illustrates
Krishna legends.

Above: Although free standing now, the innermost gopura
was once connected to an enclosure wall.
Ornate frontons embellish the doorways of the gopura
and the mandapa of the central sanctuary.

Although the temple was consecrated by Rajendravarman in 967,
it was built by Yajnavaraha, the Brahmin guru of the king.
He was a scholar, which may explain some of the shrine's
unusual features, such as the richness of the bas-relief tableaux,
lack of military scenes, meticulous details, and the
unpretentious small scale.

Above left: The depiction here of dvarapalas as slender,
relaxed youths is markedly different from the usual Khmer style.
Located in niches around the central sanctuary,
the young men hold attributes of Shiva.

Above right: The devatas are shown as voluptuous maidens,
exuding the essence of feminine beauty and fecundity,
thereby giving the shrine its modern name, Citadel of Women.

Opposite: Above the south library doorway
a chaotic scene ensues; Ravana, the demon king, shakes
Mount Kailasa (center). Shiva and his wife Uma
sit among the trees on top, and Shiva crushes the mountain
down upon Ravana with his foot.

*Above left: Nearly every inch of the exquisite central sanctuary
is covered with patterns of scrolls, intertwining foliage,
lotuses, birds, trees, mythical creatures, and* dvarapala *guardians,
all deeply and finely cut into the sandstone.*

*Above right: Although the south sanctuary had a linga inside,
scholars believe that a statue of Durga was there also.
The south false door displays charming* devatas *that grace the facades
of both sides of the sanctuaries. Yama, the god of judgment,
shown sitting on a buffalo supported by* simhas,
is both on the pediment and lintel.

*Opposite: The south library depicts Shiva legends.
The monuments were restored in the 1930s by anastylosis,
repairing defects with original materials and methods.*

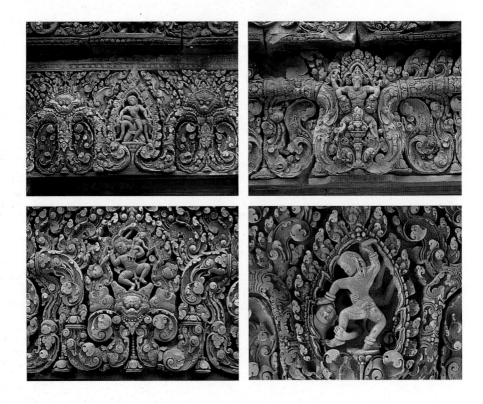

Top left: On a north tower lintel a scene of conquest unfolds;
Krishna splits the demon Kamsa. Two kalas,
magical spirits who guard entrances, emanate foliage
from their mouths.

Top right: The gopura *of the first enclosure features a lintel*
of the horse-headed god Vajimuka,
grasping the severed heads of two rakshasas.

Above left: The central sanctuary's west lintel tells the Ramayama tale
in which Ravana abducts Sita.

Above right: On a north sanctuary lintel Vishnu, in his incarnation
as Krishna, heroically severs the head of a demon.

Opposite: On a central sanctuary lintel a scene from
the Ramayama portrays the fight between Surgriva and Valin,
two monkey brothers who struggle to become king.
The hard pink sandstone has withstood harsh weather
conditions for centuries.

PHNOM
KULEN

*Early in the ninth century
Jayavarman II established his royal city
at Phnom Kulen, thereby founding
the first Khmer kingdom.
Ancient animistic spirits, neak ta,
are worshiped alongside the Buddha.*

*Below: A ninth-century Vishnu,
found among the ruins of Phnom Kulen.*

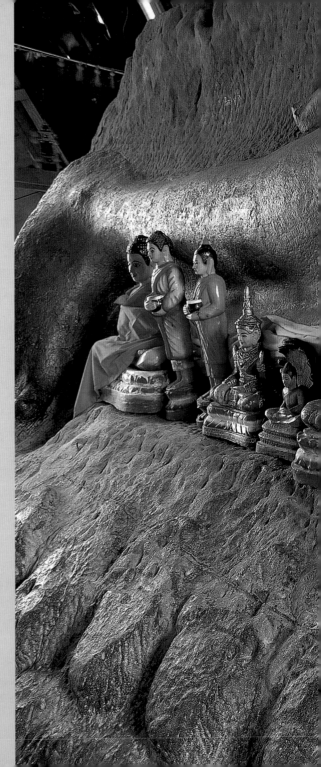

Top: *The main sources of the Siem Reap River*
are the springs that originate on Phnom Kulen.
They are worshiped with miniature houses, or khtoms,
dedicated to local spirits, the neak ta.

Above: *In 1054, a thousand lingas were carved*
by a minister of Suryavarman I into the
streambed upon the most sacred mountain in all Cambodia.
Mythologically Kulen represents the Himalaya,
the Siem Reap River, symbolizes the Ganges,
and the lingas, the sanctification of the waters by Shiva.

The largest reclining Buddha in the country
is carved from one enormous sandstone boulder located
at the 1,600-foot summit of the mountain.
It is thought to be more than nine hundred years old.

KBAL
SPEAN

Kbal Spean is near the source of the Ruisey,
a tributary of the Siem Reap River.
Numerous carvings, thought to have been
created by ascetics who lived here
during the eleventh century, are cut directly
into the hard stone of the streambed.
Here, Vishnu manifests Brahma on a lotus,
while Shiva and Parvati sit
on top of a nandi.

The universal spirit takes form as Vishnu,
who then gives birth to the god Brahma by means
of a lotus coming from his navel.

Vishnu reclines upon the serpent Ananta,
floating upon the waters of the cosmic ocean during
the creation of the universe.

BENG
MEALEA

Beng Mealea,
one of the most spectacular monuments
of the Khmer empire, was possibly
the prototype for Angkor Wat
and is only slightly smaller. It is located
near Phnom Kulen, twenty-five miles
(40 km) east of Angkor.
A pilgrim sits in front of the library
in the inner enclosure.

Top: Vaulted galleries are supported by rows of pillars

Above: Enormous blocks of bluish sandstone were cut and
fit together so tightly that even today the seams are almost undetectable.
The walls of Beng Mealea were not sculpted with bas-reliefs
but may instead have been covered with frescos.

Opposite: The shrine was constructed by Suryavarman II
in the eleventh century and was likely dedicated to Vishnu and other
Brahmanic deities. The World Monuments Fund is about to
undertake a major renovation.

PRASAT PHNOM RUNG

*Located atop an inactive volcano,
Phnom Rung has been
frequented by ascetics and holy men
since at least the seventh century.
The temple, built by Suryavarman II
in the early twelfth century,
was dedicated to Shiva.*

Above left and right: Many finely carved nagas *balustrades
line the entrance walkways. The* naga *is an ancient, highly venerated divinity
in Khmer mythology, appearing frequently in
stories of the creation and as the protector of the Buddha.*

*Opposite: The pink sandstone temple is oriented on an east-west axis,
approached by a long causeway with a succession of stairs and platforms,
culminating in a single enclosure at the summit.
The sanctuary's ornately decorated frontons depict mythological
stories from the Ramayana.*

ISSAN THAILAND:

MUANG
TAM

*Muang Tam was probably built
during the eleventh century by Jayavarman V.
This Shiva shrine is configured
with four L-shaped* sras *representing
the four oceans surrounding Mount Meru.
Outside the east entrance, large* nagas
line the sras, *their tails meeting
at small gates.*

ISSAN THAILAND:

PRASAT
PHIMAI

*In the eleventh century
Phimai was an important part
of the Khmer empire,
built at the center of the ancient city
of Vimayapura,
in an auspicious location at the
confluence of the Mun and
Klong Chakrai Rivers.
Several great Khmer kings trace
their lineage to this valley,
beginning with Jayavarman VI, who
dedicated the Buddhist shrine
in 1108.*

Top: Mahayana Buddhism had been practiced in the area
of Phimai since the seventh century,
and the sanctuary's interior iconography is Tantric.
The eastern lintel portrays the god to whom the shrine is dedicated,
Trailokyavijaya, a form of Buddha.

Above: The exterior carvings of the Phimai sanctuary were inspired by
Hindu scenes from the Ramayana.

Opposite: Phimai is one of the earliest examples of the cone-shaped,
multitiered tower that became a symbol of Khmer architecture.
It is oriented toward the south, rare in Khmer monuments, facing
the royal road leading to the capital at Angkor.

ISSAN THAILAND:

PRASAT

SIKHORAPHUM

*Sikhoraphum was built
by Suryavarman II in the twelfth century.
Above the east door of the sanctuary,
on one of the finest Khmer lintels still in situ,
a ten-armed Shiva
dances the universe into creation.*

PREAH
VIHEAR

*Preah Vihear is situated
dramatically at the summit of
the Dangkrek Mountains,
on a 1,794-foot (547 m) sandstone cliff
that overhangs the
Cambodian plains below.*

*Top: Although Preah Vihear was built over a period of
three hundred years and renovated by six kings,
Suryavarman I is credited with the major role in its construction.
The temple itself symbolizes Mount Meru as
the abode of the gods, and the ascension of the pilgrim up
the four levels is symbolic of the raising
of the levels of consciousness toward enlightenment.*

*Above: On the fourth level, the gopura opens to
a courtyard bounded by L-shaped galleries,
and a large hall leads to the gopura of the inner enclosure.
Two rows of square pillars once supported the
tiled wooden roof of the hall.*

*Opposite: The gopura of the first level is ornamented with
a triangular fronton. An unusual diamond-shaped decoration
at the top of the gable, with flower and leaf
motifs along the sides, ends in a prominent curve
with pointed finials.*

The temple was constructed of huge blocks of gray and yellow sandstone, some weighing more than five tons (3,730 kg), that were locally quarried.

From the vantage of the fourth level gopura roof,
the library and the Dangkrek Mountains may be observed.
Yasovarman I began construction of this monastic
hermitage dedicated to Shiva in the ninth century, but the site,
known as Bhavalai, was considered a sacred
pilgrimage destination long before.

Above: The two galleries forming the innermost enclosure
are curiously unconnected to the gopuras, *which are entered*
by way of two low exterior doors.
Only windows open on the courtyard, leading scholars to believe
that access to this inner sanctum was strictly limited.

Opposite: The pediment on the gopura *on the second level*
of Preah Vihear illustrates the familiar Hindu myth of creation,
The Churning of the Sea of Milk.

GEOGRAPHY AND HYDROLOGY
OF CAMBODIA

James Goodman

Many visitors to Angkor will enjoy an afternoon's boating on the Tonle Sap, or "great lake," unaware that this lake is one of nature's great wonders: during the monsoon the lake is transformed by the floodwaters of the Mekong into one of the world's largest floodplains, fed by the Tonle Sap River, the world's only "river with return" (a river that regularly reverses its flow). This extraordinary annual event is a defining attribute of a unique ecosystem created by the special geography and climate of Cambodia.

GEOGRAPHY

Cambodia, with a population of about 11 million in a land area of just over 69,000 square miles (180,000 sq km), is situated in the southwestern part of the Indochina peninsula in Southeast Asia. Bounded on the south by the Gulf of Thailand, Cambodia borders Thailand and the Lao People's Democratic Republic on the west and north and the Socialist Republic of Vietnam on the east.

Most inhabitants of Cambodia live on the Central Plains, which cover 75 percent of the land area and where the altitude is generally less than 330 feet (100 m) above sea level. The plains are surrounded by the more densely forested and sparsely populated highlands, situated along the land borders as well as the southern coast. These highlands more or less define the national borders: the Elephant Mountains, with elevations of between 1,640 and 3,300 feet (500–1000 m), and the Cardamom Mountains, rising to over 4,900 feet (1500 m), to the south and west, bordering the Gulf of Thailand; the Dangkrek Mountains, which reach elevations of between 1,640 and 2,300 feet (500–700 m), to the north, adjoining the Korat Plateau of Thailand; and, to the east, the Ratanakiri Plateau and Chhlong Highlands, which merge with the Central Highlands, of Vietnam.

CLIMATE

Cambodia, which lies entirely within the tropics, has a typical tropical climate with two distinct seasons: the monsoon season, which extends approximately from June until November, and the dry season, which lasts from December until May. The humidity is generally high year-round, but slightly lower, and more comfortable (for visitors), in December and January.

The dominant monsoon is from the Indian Ocean to the southwest. However, during El Niño years (when a shift in the dominant Pacific pressure system occurs, called the El Niño Southern Oscillation, or ENSO) this monsoon is quite weak, and typhoons of the South China

Sea monsoon system can bring additional rainfall in November and December.

Rainfall in the extensive Central Plains region during the monsoon is between 4.6 and 5.9 feet (1.4–1.8 m) on average. The eastern highlands receive up to 9.2 feet (2.8 m) annually, while the highest average rainfall, 11.8 feet (3.6 m), is recorded in the Cardamom Mountains adjacent to the Gulf of Thailand.

THE TONLE SAP BASIN AND
MEKONG LOWLANDS DRAINAGE AXIS

The drainage of the great low-lying plains, surrounded by mountains and with intense monsoon rainfall, is in itself a task of some magnitude. This drainage is further complicated by the huge additional volumes of Mekong floodwaters from the upper catchment areas in Laos, Thailand, Myanmar, China, and Tibet, which drain through Cambodia on their way to the sea. It is not surprising, therefore, that one of the dominant features of Cambodian geography is its low-lying drainage axis, which runs diagonally across the country from the northwest to the southeast: from the Tonle Sap, in the middle of the great drainage basin in the northwest of the country, via the Tonle Sap River channel, to Phnom Penh, the confluence of the Tonle Sap and the Mekong rivers. At this confluence the Mekong (and the floodwaters) turn to the southeast and, via the Mekong and Bassac River channels, drains through the lower Mekong Delta in Vietnam to discharge into the South China Sea.

During the dry season the Tonle Sap, or "great lake," the largest natural lake in Southeast Asia, is a shallow, barely navigable body of water, covering an area of approximately 1,000 square miles (2,600 sq km). Crucially, the surface elevation of the Tonle Sap at this time is more or less at sea level, measured where this drainage system meets the South China Sea 186 miles (300 km) downstream. Hence, this drainage axis could almost be described as a fjord, or an arm of the sea, that has more or less silted up. Satellite images of Cambodia during the periods of peak floods show flooding that extends widely along the length of the drainage axis, from the Mekong Delta up to Phnom Penh, on to the Tonle Sap, and beyond to the northwest, but with virtually no flooding along the course of the Mekong north of Phnom Penh.

The mechanism by which this low-lying drainage axis handles these annual monsoon floodwaters of the Mekong River at the confluence with the Tonle Sap River at Phnom Penh is unique. The Mekong River, which runs through more degrees of latitude than any other rivers apart from the Mississippi and the Nile, drains 309,000 square miles (800,000 sq m) of catchment area from its source in the Tibet Autonomous Region and in southwest China, Myanmar, Laos, and Thailand before entering Cambodia. Most of these catchments are within the monsoon belt, and the floodwaters are significant; for example, the Mekong has more or less the same naturalized flow as the Mississippi (approximately 20,000 cubic yards [15,000 cu m] of water per second), but with only a quarter of the catchment area.

The Mekong swells at the onset of the monsoon, and by mid-June the flows are too large for the two main channels south of Phnom Penh, the Mekong itself and the Bassac, to discharge the floodwaters to the delta. There is simply too much water. The land between Phnom Penh and the South China Sea is flat, which in itself hinders rapid drainage, and so drainage is impeded to the southeast. Because the water levels in the drainage axis to the northeast are lower than the levels in the flooded channels of the Mekong and Bassac Rivers below Phnom Penh, the floodwaters take the easiest path, reverse the flow of the Tonle Sap River, and enter the Tonle Sap. At this time the Tonle

Sap quadruples in size, sometimes up to 5,000 square miles (13,000 sq km), and at the height of the flooding the water level rises 23 to 30 feet (7–9 m). Records dating from 1925 confirm the extraordinary regularity of this annual event and the consistent depth of flooding, even in times of low rainfall and of drought in Cambodia. When comparing rainfall records at Angkor with those from Luang Prabang in Laos to the north (a catchment that feeds into the Mekong), records show that poor rainfall in Cambodia (during ENSO events, for example) is compensated for by heavier rainfall in catchments in Laos.

When the floodwaters crest and the channels south of Phnom Penh can carry the reduced flood volumes, the flow in the Tonle Sap River again reverses, and water flows out of the Tonle Sap Lake. This is the time when Cambodians celebrate their "water festival" with spirited boat races and poignant reflection. This annual reversal of flows is unique: the Tonle Sap River is the only "river with return" in the world, and the floodplain of this return is the largest in the world. At the end of the monsoon, the lake acts as a natural flood retention basin and slowly discharges water downstream, with beneficial results for farmers and fishermen, ultimately reducing saline ingress into the lower Mekong Delta.

The volume of silt borne in the floodwaters of the Mekong from the catchments above Cambodia is considerable. Much of this silt is deposited on the bed and the floodplain of the Tonle Sap River, immediately upstream of Phnom Penh, as the flow changes direction. The siltation processes are currently being researched, but the mechanics of sediment flow suggest that the sediment reaching the Tonle Sap is very fine, and siltation rates are lower than downstream near the great confluence. How much of the drainage axis has silted up since the Angkorian era is difficult to say. Although a regular boat service still runs for most of the year between Phnom Penh and Siem Reap, the sheer annual volume of silt is not insignificant, and the long-term process at work here is one of increasing siltation of the drainage axis to the northwest of Phnom Penh.

The fishery generated by this unique event, which creates vast flooded areas and spawning grounds, is one of the largest in Asia, providing nearly 60 percent of the annual protein intake of Cambodians. The spawning grounds for the fish lie within the band of forest immediately adjacent to the dry-season lake body, which is inundated each year by the rising waters.

THE HISTORICAL BACKGROUND
TO THE EXPLOITATION OF INLAND CAMBODIA

Exploiting this extraordinary environment was more or less forced on the Khmer people by the collapse of their Funan state sometime between the sixth and seventh centuries. This maritime state, located along the southern coast of modern Cambodia, was based on transit trade between India and China, a trade that collapsed with the development of direct ocean trade around the Malay peninsula. The end of the international maritime economy led to a political-economic shift inland, and the emergence of the "land" Chenla polity, where chiefs began to rely on control of land and labor as sources of wealth accumulation.

The Cambodian political center developed beside the Mekong River at Sambor, near Kratie in the northeast of modern Cambodia, while other small but independent Khmer chiefdoms developed elsewhere, including that of Queen Jayadevi in the Angkor region at the beginning of the eighth century. Sambor is in a flood-free zone and close to the northeastern highlands, the source of important items of international trade at the time. The migration of Jayavarman II and the Khmer elite in 770 A.D. from Sambor to the establishment of his state capitals at Angkor, on the other side of the country, at the beginning of the ninth century is one of the great enigmas of Khmer history.

The establishment of the state capitals at Angkor was contemporary with the Medieval Warm Period, when temperatures in the Northern Hemisphere, as recorded in tree rings (dendrochronologies) and farming records, were higher than at the beginning of the twenty-first century. Recent attempts at reconstructing the climate of the Angkorian era suggest that from 750 to 870 A.D. there was a period of drought in Southeast Asia. Such reconstruction relies heavily on the events in the Champa empire, the rival state situated along the south and central Vietnam coast, across the highlands from Sambor in northeast Cambodia. The Chams moved their capital south, to a different climate zone, at the mouth of the Mekong in 750 A.D. but returned to their original capital near present day Da Nang in 870 A.D. At the same time there is a complete break in the epigraphic corpus over this period in Cambodia, which suggests that the move to Angkor was, at the least, a period of stress and probably a move to ensure survival. The subsequent Khmer aggrandizement and empire is testament to the extraordinary prescience of the elite in response to crisis.

THE SITE AT ANGKOR

The Tonle Sap Lake, at the northwestern end of the drainage axis, is relatively protected from the more turbulent ebb and flow of the annual drainage dramas caused by the Mekong floodwaters downstream. The location of Angkor in the ninth century offered many advantages: transportation routes on the Tonle Sap and the river system of Cambodia; a superb fishery; high ground above the floodplain closer to the lake than any other location; at least one perennial river, the Siem Reap, flowing from the Kulen Hills north of Angkor, to the Tonle Sap; building materials and, in the sands of the Angkor plain, reasonable foundation material for their temple complexes.

Most important of all, however, were the additional rice-cropping opportunities offered by the lake itself, opportunities that were independent of the local rainfall. The ancient floating rice varieties growing in the rising waters of the Tonle Sap and the crop grown on the floodplain at the end of the monsoon provided food security when rainfall was insufficient for the rain-fed crop. When rainfall was plenty, the state enjoyed an agricultural surplus. The rain-fed crop is grown on the sandy plain above the floodplain that surrounds the lake and harvested in December–January of each year. The same crops are grown around Angkor today as reported by the celebrated Chinese diplomat Chou Ta-kuan in A.D. 1296–97.

Nowadays, of course, many of the traditional varieties of rice have been replaced by modern, nonphotoperiod-sensitive rice varieties that can be grown at any time of the year. The traditional *Indica* rice species of the tropics is photoperiod-sensitive, with most varieties maturing at the same time of the year irrespective of planting. So the introduction to Cambodia of the quick ripening, photosensitive *Indica* varieties that emerged in Champa during the first through sixth centuries A.D. allowed another crop to be sown on the floodplain at the end of the monsoon. These new varieties were fundamental to the much wider spread of rice cultivation throughout Asia, and of course crucial to the flowering of the Khmer empire. Such varieties were able to emerge in the Champa state because of the quite different climate regimes within the Champa orbit; in the south, around the mouth of the Mekong Delta, a six-month rainfall pattern prevails, while in the north, near present day Da Nang, the monsoon climate is of much shorter duration but with far higher intensities.

THE BARAYS AT ANGKOR

Following the move to Angkor, the Khmers constructed a number of structures over the next 300 years (Indratataka, c. A.D. 800; East Baray, c. 890; West Baray, c. 1040; North Baray, c. 1190) that are generally described as *barays* (reservoirs created not by excavation but by the raising of large encircling dykes). The largest *baray*, the West Baray, which is adjacent to the airport, is a staggering feat of engineering measuring five by two miles (8 by 3 km), with dykes over 33 feet (10 m) high; modern rules of thumb for manual labor suggest that it would have taken 40,000 people over three years to construct this *baray*.

In the absence of any relevant records, the function of these vast *barays* has been the subject of considerable debate, broadly split between engineers and nonengineers; the latter now increasingly use new tools, such as satellite imagery, to attempt to determine the hydrology of the past.

The conventional interpretation of these structures at Angkor, and the interpretation provided by most tourist guides, is that they were part of an hydraulic system capable of producing two to three crops of rice a year in an irrigation network extending between the Angkor capital and the floodplain. Bernard-Philippe Groslier, the last director of the Ecole Française d'Extrême Orient (EFEO) and conservator of the Angkor Conservancy in the 1960s and early '70s, proposed a "citie hydraulique" that was the first city in history of over 1 million people, fed almost exclusively by the produce from a massive and sophisticated irrigation system.

Recent engineering studies, however, tend to support the earlier interpretation by the irrigation engineer W. J. van Liere in reports to the Mekong River Commission in the 1960s that irrigation is not practical in the sandy ground around Angkor. Irrigation is barely practiced in modern Cambodia, and if the claim for irrigation over the six centuries of the Angkorian era is valid, the loss of such a culture would be surprising.

Two recent studies of the groundwater regime in the Angkor plain, one to investigate how to supply water to meet the demands of the huge increase in tourism since 1998, the other to investigate restoring water to the reflecting ponds of the Neak Pean temple complex in the middle of the North Baray, are of particular relevance. The wells drilled to monitor groundwater show an almost uniform geology throughout the archaeological area. There is a 50- to 66-foot (13–20 m) layer of sand at the geological surface that rests on sandstone. The groundwater is very close to the surface in this sand layer and is free to move, rising and falling over the annual cycle by an average of 8 feet (2.5 m). During the monsoon the ground is generally flooded, producing ideal conditions for growing rice.

It is most likely that the modern groundwater conditions are essentially similar to conditions during the Angkorian era, as there is no evidence of formal and historic wells anywhere throughout the successive state capitals in the historic site of Angkor. The Chinese diplomat Chou Ta-kuan noted in A.D. 1296–97 the Khmer practice of regular bathing (up to twice a day in the hot season) in the family ponds that were everywhere. Customs are remarkably similar now; every family appears to have a pond in the yard, and shallow wells are used extensively. An interesting social aspect of such a benign water environment is the public health benefits afforded by a series of separate ponds, which are fed by groundwater rather than streams and channels. The sandy ground acts as a giant sand filter, containing any waterborne disease.

THE ROLE OF THE BARAYS

The *barays* are all located on the plain above the extended Tonle Sap floodplain, which is uniformly sand. Sand is generally an impractical foundation for water-retaining reservoirs, and there is no evidence to date of any impermeable layers within the *barays* themselves to provide water-retention capability. In this harsh tropical climate, with an extreme annual cycle of flooding and drying, it is notable that after 800 years there is remarkably little obvious settlement in any of the immense temple structures that comprise Angkor, the reason being that there is very little underlying clay anywhere in the archaeological area.

Recent and detailed mapping of the Angkor Conservancy area, supported by additional field surveys, has allowed a reassessment of the *barays*. Contrary to the conventional interpretation, only the West Baray is a true *baray*. The ground levels in the other *barays* are lower than the surrounding area, showing that they would appear to have been excavated. This finding challenges the argument that the demise of the irrigation system, if not the empire itself, was due to siltation in the reservoirs and a collapse of the irrigation arrangements.

In this context, where water tables are close to the surface throughout the year, excavating ground allows an open water surface to be maintained for a longer period after the end of the monsoon, when the groundwater levels start to fall. This could have allowed a crop of rice, but the available areas, while vast for reservoirs, are small for rice cropping. Alternative crops are more likely, such as the medicinally important lotus, which was also extensively cultivated in the contemporary and neighboring Thai state as well as in India where it was considered an essential drought security crop.

The West Baray is located topographically in the lowest area of the archaeological area, and even without the modern diversion of the Siem Reap River, it would hold water longer than any of the other *barays*. Ak Yum, a pre-Angkorian temple complex, which is also generally accepted as one of the sites of the first capitals of Jayavarman II, is located in the southern dyke of this baray. Satellite images of the A.D. 2000 floods show that, despite an extensive array of modern embankments to the south, this area is vulnerable to flooding. The likely interpretation is that the dykes of this baray were originally flood protection dykes, which were formalized into the dykes of the *baray* in the middle of the eleventh century, as part of an overall plan based on the Hindu mythological geography of Mount Meru, the abode of the gods, surrounded by oceans (represented by the *barays* and the Tonle Sap to the south).

THE CLIMATE AND THE CONSTRUCTION CAMPAIGNS

The Khmer state was capable of mobilizing large labor forces in their construction campaigns, as witness, for example, the massive earthmoving involved in the dykes of the West Baray. Supporting the vast teams of craftsmen, artisans, and labor whose skills are displayed in the magnificent temples would have required an altogether more significant agricultural, or economic, surplus.

The Angkorian era was contemporary with the Medieval Warm Period, a time of great changes in the climate in many parts of the world. The original migration of the elite to Angkor was, as discussed, probably climate related, and research on reconstructing the historic climate is particularly interesting.

The surviving epigraphic records on stone stelae give the dates of the consecration of the principal divinities of the particular temples. Clearly, many of the temple complexes exhibit a variety of styles that have yet to be correctly interpreted, so it is impossible to be certain whether the consecration dates record reconstruction, rehabilitation of existing structures, or indeed entirely new construction. Bearing this in mind, it is interesting to note that construction does not appear to be continuous or uniform during the six centuries of the Angkorian era. The distinct periods of construction must also have been periods of economic surplus, which implies good harvests.

Incredibly, over half of all the Khmer monumental construction is attributed to the reign of Jayavarman VII, in the latter part of the twelfth century, including a vast network of roads and hospitals. His capital at Preah Khan at Angkor was contemporary with some remarkable edifices some distance from Angkor, such as Banteay Chhmar to the northwest and Beng Mealea to the east.

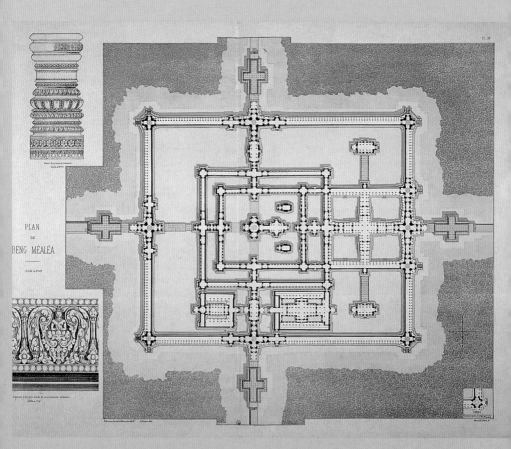

Beng Mealea floor plan by Louis Delaporte. Published in 1914-1924.

Climate reconstructions for Southeast Asia during the Angkorian era is possible because contemporary climate records from elsewhere in the world can be related to Southeast Asia by recent work on El Niño Southern Oscillation (ENSO) events. This research identifies those geographic areas that respond in the same way, either wetter or drier, to ENSO events. These teleconnections, as they are called, show that conditions elsewhere in the world during the ninth century were drier than normal years. These conditions have been confirmed by the migrations in Southeast Asia of Champa power to the south of Vietnam and of the Khmer elite to the northwest of Cambodia, apparently to avoid drought conditions.

In the twelfth century studies of oak tree rings in lowland Germany, of Nile gauge readings of winter stages in Cairo (recording rainfall in the highlands of East Africa) and of written records in South India, Korea, and Honshu show—all these telecommunications were very much wetter than they are today. The teleconnection implication is that Southeast Asia must also have been wetter. Such conditions would have provided the agricultural surplus necessary for the largest construction program ever undertaken during the life of a king, Jayavarman VII.

The migration, settlement, and flowering of the Khmer state at Angkor is a story of success and a tribute to visionary state planning. Faced with some adversity, probably an extended period of drought, the elite abandoned their capital and moved across the country to harness the unique environment at Angkor with novel exploitation of the available water resources. Despite clear setbacks, including abandonment of Angkor entirely early in the tenth century, the Khmer state flourished.

NATIONAL MUSEUM
OF CAMBODIA

Top: *The National Museum of Cambodia,
which houses the greatest collection of Khmer art and artifacts
in the world, was designed with traditional elements
by Georges Groslier in 1916.*

Above: *An exhibit of Buddhas includes
rare examples made of wood from Angkor Wat.*

SCULPTURE
FROM THE NATIONAL MUSEUM AND
ANGKOR CONSERVANCY

Vishnu
6th c; Phnom Da,
Angkor Borei, Ta Keo;
schist

Yoni Receptacle
second half 6th c;
Angkor Borei, Ta Keo;
schist

Vishnu
second half 6th c; Prei Veng;
sandstone

Durga Mahishasuramardini
beginning 7th c;
Sambor Prei Kuk, Kompong Thom;
sandstone

Durga Mahishasuramardini
7th–8th c; Prei Veng;
sandstone

Harihara
late 8th c–early 9th c;
Trapong Phong;
sandstone

Guardian with Monkey Head
10th c; Banteay Srei;
sandstone

Buddha and Naga
second half 11th c;
Kompong Cham;
sandstone

Lokesvara
12th c; Angkor Thom,
Gate of the Dead;
sandstone

Jayavarman VII
late 12th c;
Angkor Thom, Krol Romeas;
sandstone

Jayavarman VII
second half of 12th c;
Preah Khan, Preah Vihear;
sandstone

Buddha
13th c; Bayon;
sandstone

Buddhist Boundary Post
13th–14th c;
Bos Prah Nan, Kompong Cham;
sandstone

Naga and Garuda
date unknown;
Angkor Conservancy;
sandstone

Lotus Bud
date unknown;
Angkor Conservancy;
sandstone

AFTERWORD

PRESERVATION OF
THE CULTURAL HERITAGE
OF ANGKOR

Kerya Chau Sun
Director of Angkor Tourist Development, APSARA

A ngkor, capitol of the Khmer empire from the ninth to the fifteenth centuries, is first and foremost the precious cultural heritage of the Khmer people and a symbol of Khmer identity. Angkor not only designates a geographical region with its remarkable monumental and artistic artifacts but, more importantly, represents a dynamic cultural complex that profoundly penetrates all aspects of Khmer society extending beyond national boundaries.

Following a twenty-year period of war and neglect, King Norodom Sihanouk publicly declared that Angkor was in danger, launching an appeal for its safeguarding. The international community responded positively, and in December 1991 the site was included on the World Heritage List. The royal government of Cambodia was given three years to create an authority empowered to take charge of the protection and conservation of the sites and ensure its responsible management. Once this condition was met, the World Heritage Committee gave permanent status to the classification of the Angkor temples, which includes the monuments surrounding Angkor as well as the Roluos group and the temple of Banteay Srei. Many other monuments in Siem Reap Province could not be listed because of their inaccessibility at the time and the impossibility of giving them adequate protection.

Back in the 1960s, when Cambodia's economy was reasonably self-sufficient, King Norodom Sihanouk felt that no special emphasis should be put on tourism, and that the number of visitors to Angkor should be kept low so as to preserve Angkor. But how can we say no to mass tourism, as a fast-track revenue solution for a war-traumatized people whose income is among the lowest in the world? How can Cambodians resist the temptation to make money quickly?

Tourism in Cambodia must first and foremost be culturally sensitive, with specific goals that prevent it from becoming overcommercialized, which would give rise to rapid and ill conceived development. Tourism is a necessary partner, but its power to overwhelm must be channeled. This means clearly understanding the effect of the industry upon traditional cultures thrust into the twenty-first century. Enhancement of the services offered would give visitors an incentive to stay longer, and the quality of the infrastructure would have considerable impact on Angkor's long-term appeal as a tourist site. Implementation of a policy for tourism development is most challenging.

To achieve its goals, Cambodia has set up a number of support mechanisms.

The Angkor site was included permanently on the World Heritage List in 1995. This status is monitored by the International Coordinating Committee for the Safeguarding and Development of the Historic Site of Angkor, which has been meeting three times a year since 1993 to oversee the security and development of the site. The two co-chairs of this committee are France and Japan, the leading donors to the rehabilitation of the Angkor site. UNESCO provides the services of standing secretariat, while the APSARA Authority represents Cambodia.

The APSARA Authority was created by royal decree in 1995 to protect and develop the historical site of Angkor, with emphasis on planned tourism that respects and supports Khmer culture. The activities of its three aligned departments are clearly in keeping with its mandate:

¶ The Urban Development Department controls urban planning and construction in the Angkor/Siem Reap region, in compliance with zoning laws, and in liaison with the Ministry of Land Planning, Urban Development and Construction.

¶ The Culture and Monuments Department is responsible for maintenance and security of the monuments, in liaison with the Ministry of Culture.

¶ The Tourism Development Department plans, regulates, and controls the flow of tourists, in liaison with the Ministry of Tourism.

Short-term objectives are no longer enough; foresight is needed for proper adaptation to needs in the mid- and long term. For Cambodia, preservation tourism is the byword: nature has an intrinsic value that can never be replaced, and our heritage must be seen as a legacy received, protected, and passed on. There must be solidarity among the generations—past, present, and future—to take full responsibility for the management and preservation of Cambodia's unique natural and cultural heritage.

CHRONOLOGY OF SITES

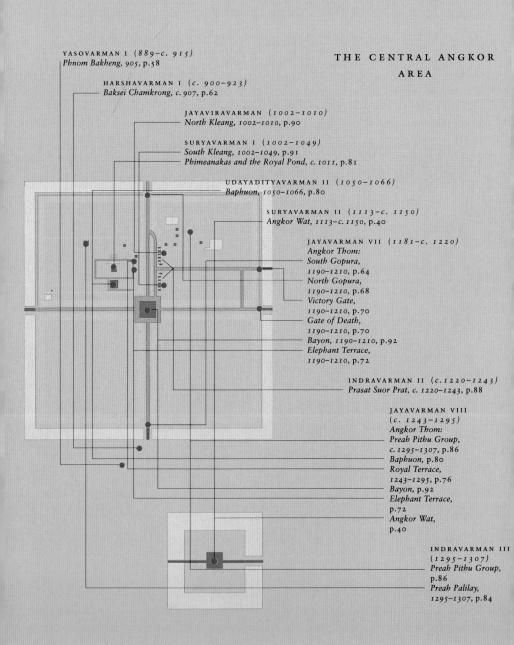

YASOVARMAN I *(889–c. 915)*
Phnom Bakheng, 905, p.58

THE CENTRAL ANGKOR
AREA

HARSHAVARMAN I *(c. 900–923)*
Baksei Chamkrong, c. 907, p.62

JAYAVIRAVARMAN *(1002–1010)*
North Kleang, 1002–1010, p.90

SURYAVARMAN I *(1002–1049)*
South Kleang, 1002–1049, p.91
Phimeanakas and the Royal Pond, c. 1011, p.81

UDAYADITYAVARMAN II *(1050–1066)*
Baphuon, 1050–1066, p.80

SURYAVARMAN II *(1113–c. 1150)*
Angkor Wat, 1113–c.1150, p.40

JAYAVARMAN VII *(1181–c. 1220)*
Angkor Thom:
South Gopura,
1190–1210, p.64
North Gopura,
1190–1210, p.68
Victory Gate,
1190–1210, p.70
Gate of Death,
1190–1210, p.70
Bayon, 1190–1210, p.92
Elephant Terrace,
1190–1210, p.72

INDRAVARMAN II *(c.1220–1243)*
Prasat Suor Prat, c. 1220–1243, p.88

JAYAVARMAN VIII
(c. 1243–1295)
Angkor Thom:
Preah Pithu Group,
c. 1295–1307, p.86
Baphuon, p.80
Royal Terrace,
1243–1295, p.76
Bayon, p.92
Elephant Terrace,
p.72
Angkor Wat,
p.40

INDRAVARMAN III
(1295–1307)
Preah Pithu Group,
p.86
Preah Palilay,
1295–1307, p.84

800 A.D.   850   900   950   1000   1050   1100   1150   1200   1250   1300   1350   14

THE TEMPLES

SURROUNDING ANGKOR

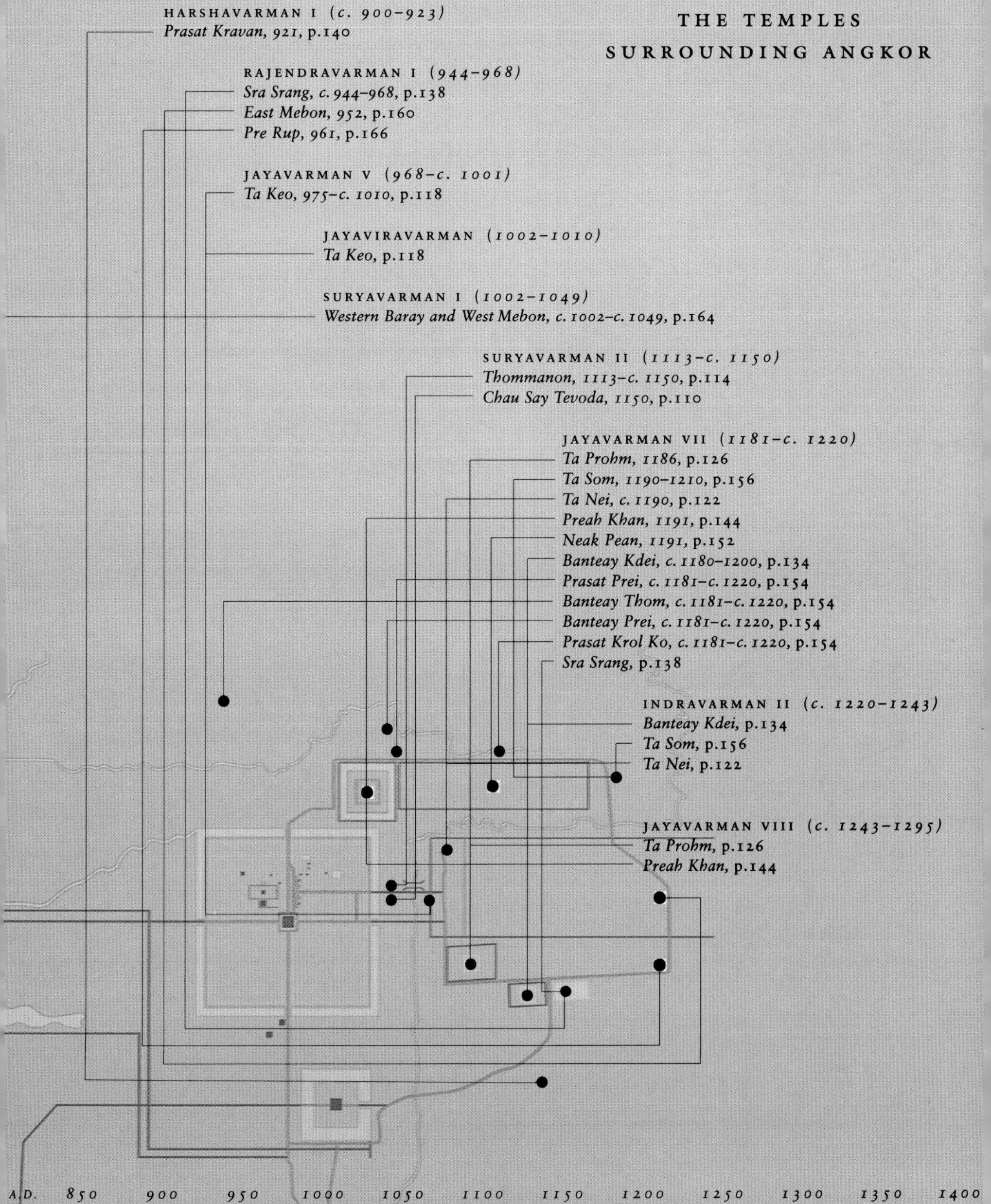

HARSHAVARMAN I *(c. 900–923)*
— *Prasat Kravan, 921, p.140*

RAJENDRAVARMAN I *(944–968)*
— *Sra Srang, c. 944–968, p.138*
— *East Mebon, 952, p.160*
— *Pre Rup, 961, p.166*

JAYAVARMAN V *(968–c. 1001)*
— *Ta Keo, 975–c. 1010, p.118*

JAYAVIRAVARMAN *(1002–1010)*
— *Ta Keo, p.118*

SURYAVARMAN I *(1002–1049)*
— *Western Baray and West Mebon, c. 1002–c. 1049, p.164*

SURYAVARMAN II *(1113–c. 1150)*
— *Thommanon, 1113–c. 1150, p.114*
— *Chau Say Tevoda, 1150, p.110*

JAYAVARMAN VII *(1181–c. 1220)*
— *Ta Prohm, 1186, p.126*
— *Ta Som, 1190–1210, p.156*
— *Ta Nei, c. 1190, p.122*
— *Preah Khan, 1191, p.144*
— *Neak Pean, 1191, p.152*
— *Banteay Kdei, c. 1180–1200, p.134*
— *Prasat Prei, c. 1181–c. 1220, p.154*
— *Banteay Thom, c. 1181–c. 1220, p.154*
— *Banteay Prei, c. 1181–c. 1220, p.154*
— *Prasat Krol Ko, c. 1181–c. 1220, p.154*
— *Sra Srang, p.138*

INDRAVARMAN II *(c. 1220–1243)*
— *Banteay Kdei, p.134*
— *Ta Som, p.156*
— *Ta Nei, p.122*

JAYAVARMAN VIII *(c. 1243–1295)*
— *Ta Prohm, p.126*
— *Preah Khan, p.144*

A.D.   850   900   950   1000   1050   1100   1150   1200   1250   1300   1350   1400

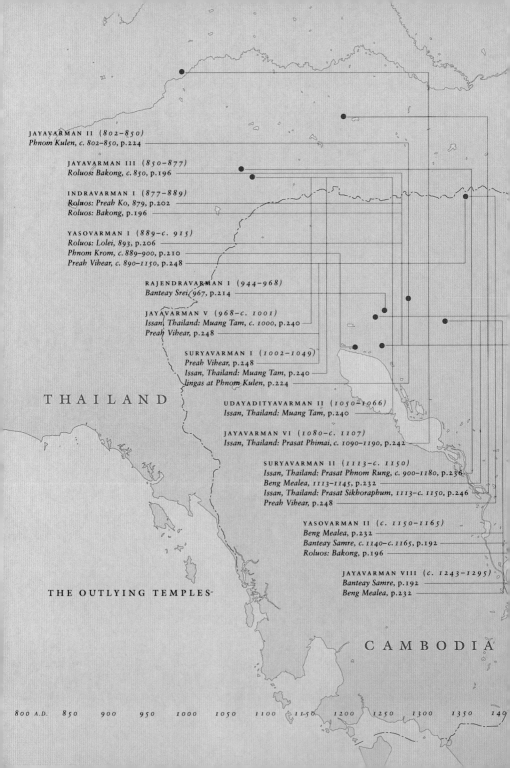

JAYAVARMAN II (802–850)
Phnom Kulen, c. 802–850, p.224

JAYAVARMAN III (850–877)
Roluos: Bakong, c. 850, p.196

INDRAVARMAN I (877–889)
Roluos: Preah Ko, 879, p.202
Roluos: Bakong, p.196

YASOVARMAN I (889–c. 915)
Roluos: Lolei, 893, p.206
Phnom Krom, c. 889–900, p.210
Preah Vihear, c. 890–1150, p.248

RAJENDRAVARMAN I (944–968)
Banteay Srei, 967, p.214

JAYAVARMAN V (968–c. 1001)
Issan, Thailand: Muang Tam, c. 1000, p.240
Preah Vihear, p.248

SURYAVARMAN I (1002–1049)
Preah Vihear, p.248
Issan, Thailand: Muang Tam, p.240
lingas at Phnom Kulen, p.224

THAILAND

UDAYADITYAVARMAN II (1050–1066)
Issan, Thailand: Muang Tam, p.240

JAYAVARMAN VI (1080–c. 1107)
Issan, Thailand: Prasat Phimai, c. 1090–1190, p.242

SURYAVARMAN II (1113–c. 1150)
Issan, Thailand: Prasat Phnom Rung, c. 900–1180, p.236
Beng Mealea, 1113–1145, p.232
Issan, Thailand: Prasat Sikhoraphum, 1113–c. 1150, p.246
Preah Vihear, p.248

YASOVARMAN II (c. 1150–1165)
Beng Mealea, p.232
Banteay Samre, c. 1140–c. 1165, p.192
Roluos: Bakong, p.196

JAYAVARMAN VIII (c. 1243–1295)
Banteay Samre, p.192
Beng Mealea, p.232

THE OUTLYING TEMPLES

CAMBODIA

800 A.D.   850   900   950   1000   1050   1100   1150   1200   1250   1300   1350   140

FLOOR PLANS

The floor plans on pages 273-275 are not all reproduced on the same scale.

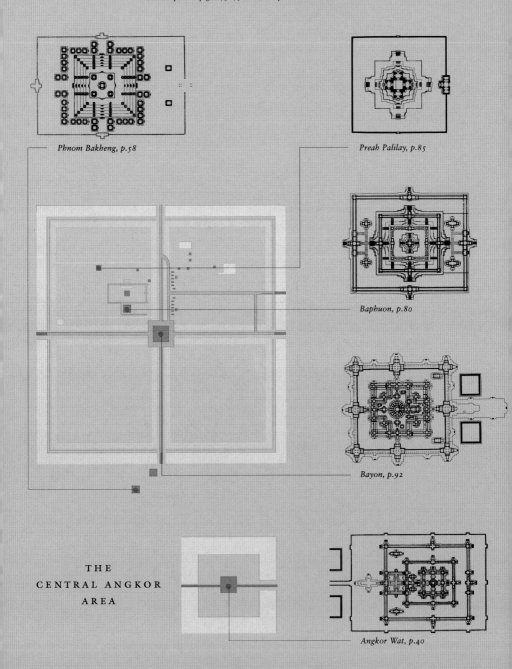

Phnom Bakheng, p.58

Preah Palilay, p.85

Baphuon, p.80

Bayon, p.92

THE
CENTRAL ANGKOR
AREA

Angkor Wat, p.40

THE TEMPLES
SURROUNDING ANGKOR

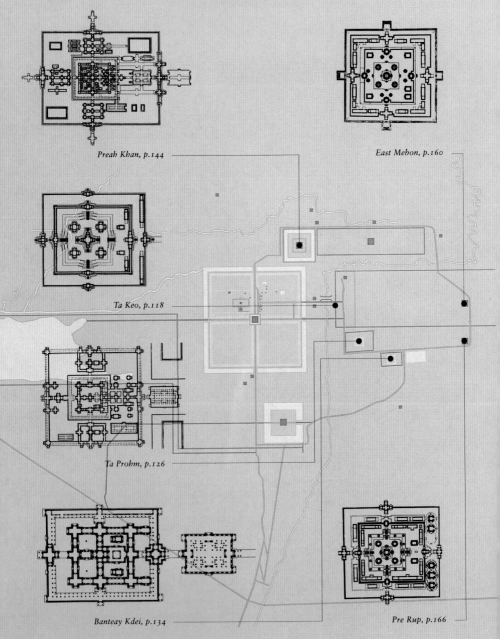

Preah Khan, p.144

East Mebon, p.160

Ta Keo, p.118

Ta Prohm, p.126

Banteay Kdei, p.134

Pre Rup, p.166

THAILAND

CAMBODIA

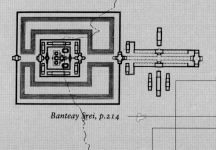

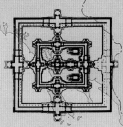

Banteay Srei, p.214

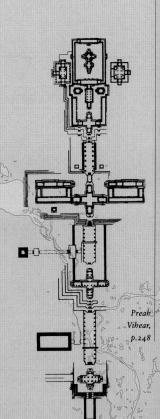

Banteay Samre, p.192

Preah Vihear, p.248

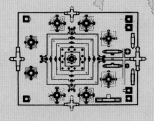

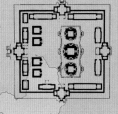

Roluos: Bakong, p.196

Phnom Krom, p.210

GLOSSARY

Key: *(B)* Buddhist, *(Ch)* Chinese, *(Gr)* Greek, *(H)* Hindu, *(Kh)* Khmer, *(L)* Latin, *(S)* Sanskrit, *(Th)* Thai

Agni *(H)* Vedic god of fire; sacrificial fire

Airavata *(H)* Multiheaded elephant; mount of the god Indra

Altar Raised platform on which offerings are made to an ancestor or god

Amrita *(H)* Elixir of life produced by the Churning of the celestial Milky Ocean

Ananta *(H)* Serpent god; the endless; also called Sesa and Vasuki

Anastylosis Restoration of a building by disassembling it, numbering and cataloguing the pieces, and reassembling it in a structurally sound form, using as many original materials as possible

Angkor *(Kh)* From the Sanskrit word *nagara*, capital city

Antechamber Smaller room leading into a larger room

Antefix Decorative detail added to the eaves of a roof or parapet; in Khmer architecture, often shaped like a miniature tower, *garuda*, or *naga*

Apsara *(H, S)* Celestial nymph; female divinity who dances for the gods

Ascetic *(H)* Religious seeker who practices austerities

Asura *(H)* Demon with godlike powers; enemy of the gods

Avalokitesvara *(B)* Bodhisattva of compassion in Mahayana Buddhism; also known as Lokesvara

Avatara *(H, S)* Reincarnation of a god on earth, especially of Vishnu

Bai kriem *(Kh)* Grilled rice; Khmer word for laterite

Balaha *(B)* Mythical horse who saved Simhala

Bali *(H)* King of the demons

Baluster Circular post or pillar that supports a rail forming a balustrade

Balustrade Railing

Banteay *(Kh)* Fortress, citadel; temple with enclosure walls

Baray *(S)* Artificial reservoir; lake

Bas-relief Carving in which figures project only slightly from the background; a sculpture in low relief

Beng *(Kh)* Pond, pool

Bodhi *(B)* Enlightenment; tree *(Ficus religiosus)* under which Buddha reached enlightenment

Bodhisattva *(B, S)* Future Buddha in Mahayana Buddhism; being who forestalls his own Nirvana in order to teach and help others

Brahma *(H, S)* First of Hindu trinity of gods; creator of the universe; sometimes appears with four heads to look in all directions

Buddha *(B, S)* The Awakened One; Gautama Siddhartha, born about 543 B.C.

Causeway Raised path across a body of water leading to a temple entrance

Cella *(L)* Inner chamber of the central sanctuary; the *garba griha*

Chakra *(B)* Wheel, symbol of the law of dharma and the Buddhist doctrine

Chakra *(H)* a center of psychic or physical energy

Chakravartin *(H, S)* Legendary emperor of the universe; universal sovereign

Cham Inhabitants of Champa, Indianized kingdom in Vietnam that flourished from the 2nd to the 15th century

Chedi *(B)* Stupa, a funerary monument

Chenla *(Ch)* Chinese name for early Cambodia

Citadel Fortress on a commanding height; stronghold, refuge

Colonette Small column on each side of a door

Concentricity Having a common center; in Khmer architecture, the central sanctuary is surrounded by enclosure walls and a moat.

Corbelled vault False arch built of corbels

Cornice Curved or overhanging architectural element above the lintel or wall

Cruciform In the shape of a cross

Damrei *(H, Kh)* Elephant

Deva *(H)* God or deity; spiritual being

Devaraja *(H, S)* The god who is king; Siva cult that evolved into Khmer succession of god-kings

Devata *(H, S)* General term for female divinity

Devi *(H)* Consort of Siva; also known as Uma, Gauri, and Parvati

Dharma *(H, B)* In Hinduism, duty or law; the Buddhist doctrine

Dharmsala *(H)* Shelter for pilgrims

Durga *(H, S)* One of the wives of Shiva in her terrible forms

Dvarapala *(H, S)* Deity; temple guardian

Enclosure Area surrounded by a wall or fence

Enlightenment *(H)* Freedom from the cycle of rebirth; the ultimate spiritual goal of Hinduism and Buddhism

False door Decorative door that doesn't open; in Khmer architecture, made of stone carved to mimic wood

Flying palace Celestial palace of the gods

Frieze Horizontal band usually decorated with sculpture

Fronton Triangular-shaped façade that contains the pediment and increases the upper portion of a building above the door; often decorated with narrative scenes from Hindu mythology

Funan *(Ch)* Chinese name for Indianized kingdom that preceded Angkor

Gable Triangular architectural feature

Gajasimha *(H)* Mythical lion with a snout

Gallery Covered porch or walkway, open on one side, supported by pillars

Gandharva *(H)* Celestial musician

Ganesh *(H, S)* God of wisdom, remover of obstacles; elephant-headed son of Shiva and Parvati

Ganga *(H, S)* Second wife of Siva

Ganges *(H)* Sacred river of northern India

Garba griha *(H, S)* Cella; inner chamber of the central sanctuary

Garuda *(H)* Mythical vehicle of Vishnu; divine bird with arms and torso of a man, and beak, wings, and claws of an eagle

Gopura *(H, S)* Entrance pavilion, often with tower

Guru *(H)* Spiritual master

Hamsa *(H, S)* Mythical sacred goose; mount of Brahma; symbol of asceticism

Hanuman *(H, S)* Monkey god; chief of army of monkeys; faithful servant of Rama

Harihara *(H, S)* Hindu deity with attributes of Vishnu and Shiva

Hayagriva *(H)* Vishnu in the form of a horse

Himavatta *(H)* Mythological forest surrounding Mount Meru

Hinayana Buddhism *(B)* Lesser Vehicle; Theriveda, or the southern school of an early form of Buddhism

Indra *(H, S)* Vedic god of the sky, storms, war; guardian of the east

Indrajit *(H)* Character in *Ramayana*; son of Ravana

Jataka *(B, S)* Birth stories of the former lives of Buddha

Jaya *(H, S)* Victory

Juxtaposition Side by side; in Khmer architecture, sanctuaries attached to each other, or an annex attached to a sanctuary

Kala *(H, S)* Protector divinity of the temple; monster with bulging eyes; time; death; black

Kaliya *(H)* Mythical *naga* subdued by Krishna

Kalpa *(H)* Hindu cycle of time; one day and one night of Brahma

Kama *(H)* God of love

Karma *(H, S)* An act and its results

Khmer Synonymous with Cambodian culture

King of Ayodhya *(H)* Character in *Ramayana*

Ko *(Kh)* Bull, ox

Kompong *(Kh)* Village or wharf

Krishna *(H, S)* Incarnation of Vishnu; the cowherd; hero in *Mahabharata*

Kubera *(H)* God of wealth; guardian of the north

Kurma *(H)* Incarnation of Vishnu as giant turtle; supports Mount Mandara in the Churning of the Milky Ocean

Kurukshetra *(H)* Location of the great war in *Mahabharata*

Laksmana *(H)* Character in *Ramayana*; brother of Rama

Laksmi *(H, S)* Wife of Vishnu; goddess of beauty, good fortune, and wealth; emblem is the lotus

Lanka *(H)* Island of Ceylon; kingdom ruled by Ravana; mythological home of the Rakshasas

Laterite *(L)* Soft, porous, iron-rich rock that is easily cut and becomes very hard upon exposure to the sun

Library Small buildings on either side of the entrance to a temple, probably for sacred texts or perhaps to house the sacred fire; exact use debated

Linga, or **lingum** *(H, S)* Phallus; symbol of Shiva; sign, symbol of the creative power of the universe

Lintel Block resting on door pillars, spanning the entrance

Lokapala *(B)* Protector of the world, guardian of the four directions or cardinal points

Lokesvara *(B, S)* Lord of the world; Bodhisattva of compassion; a form of Avalokitesvara

Mahayana Buddhism *(B, S)* The Great Vehicle; northern school of a later form of Buddhism

Mahout *(H)* Man who controls an elephant

Maitreya *(B)* A future Buddha

Makara *(H, S)* Mythical sea animal with body of a reptile, claws of a bird of prey, and head with elephant's trunk, often emanating *nagas*

Mandala *(H)* Circle, magic diagram, sacred representation of the cosmos and consciousness

Mandapa *(H, S)* Antechamber; vestibule that leads to the main shrine

Mandara *(H, S)* In Hindu mythology, mountain of riches; used to churn the Milky Ocean in creation myth

Mara *(H, B)* Evil spirit who tempted Buddha

Marica *(H)* Character in *Ramayana*

Maya *(H)* The measuring out or displaying of forms; the illusion of reality created in Brahma's dreams

Moat Ditch filled with water, surrounding a fortress, castle, or Khmer temple

Moksha *(H)* Liberation from death and the cycle of rebirths

Mon People of lower Myanmar and central Thailand

Mount Kailasa *(H)* Remote peak in western Tibet and celestial home of Shiva; most important place of pilgrimage for Hindus and Buddhists

Mount Meru *(H)* Mythical mountain at the center of the universe; celestial home of the gods; identified with Mount Kailasa in western Tibet

Mucilinda *(H, B)* Mythical *naga* in the form of a cobra that sheltered the Buddha in meditation

Mudra *(H, S)* Ritual hand gesture

Mukkuta Conical headpiece worn by an asura; tiara or diadem

Naga *(H, S)* Stylized cobra; ancient multiheaded serpent deity; protector of riches; symbol of water

Nagara *(H, S)* Capital city

Nagaraja *(H, S)* King of the *nagas*

Nandi *(H, S)* Sacred bull, mount of Shiva

Narasimha *(H)* Incarnation of Vishnu with lower half human, upper half lion

Neak Ta *(Kh)* Local deity or nature spirit

Nirvana *(H, S)* The blowing out; extinction of the Self; enlightenment

Pagoda *(H, S)* Building used to house sacred images; temple

Pala *(H, S)* Guardian

Pali *(B)* Language of the Buddhist canon written in Sri Lanka during the first century B.C.

Parinirvana *(B)* Buddha's entry into Nirvana, represented as a reclining Buddha

Parvati *(H, S)* Goddess consort of Shiva; daughter of the mountain; also known as Uma, Gauri, and Devi

Pedestal Bottom support of a column or statue; base or foundation

Pediment Triangular portion above the door; includes the tympanum and the arch above

Phnom *(Kh)* Hill, mount

Pilaster Shallow rectangular column projecting only slightly from a wall, with a base, shaft, and capital

Pillar Strong vertical support for a superstructure; column

Polychrome Referring to the use of multiple colors

Porch Covered entrance to a building

Portico Entrance porch

Pradaksina *(B)* Circumambulation path, keeping the sacred monument or object always to the right

Prasat *(H, S)* Sanctuary in the shape of a tower; center of the temple

Preah *(Kh)* Holy, sacred

Prei *(Kh)* Forest

Quincunx Arrangement of five objects, one in the center, the others in the four corners surrounding it, like five dots on a die

Rahu *(H, S)* Demon cut by Vishnu's disc; causes eclipses by swallowing moon and sun

Raksasa *(H)* Demon; character in *Ramayana*

Rama *(H, S)* Avatar of Vishnu; king and hero in *Ramayana*

Rati *(H)* Goddess of love, sexual desire; wife of Kama

Ravana *(H)* Demon; multiheaded, many-armed ruler of Lanka; character in *Ramayana*

Redenting Cutting or reducing the angles of the edge of a square structure to create a curved shape; in Khmer architecture, used to round towers into cone shapes

Rishi *(H)* Hindu sage, ascetic, holy man

Sakyamuni *(B)* Sage of the Sakya clan; the Buddha

Samsara *(H)* Cycle of birth, death, and rebirth

Sanctuary Holy place or building set aside for worship; refuge

Sanskrit *(H)* Sacred language and script of India; language of Mahayana texts

Sarong *(H)* Length of fabric wrapped around the lower body

Sema *(B)* Buddhist boundary stone

Sesa *(H)* Serpent god; also called Ananta and Vasuki

Shakti, or **Sakti** *(H)* Goddess; divine female creative energy

Shiva, or **Siva(s)** *(H, S)* Patron god of ascetics, the auspicious; creator and destroyer of the Universe; third god in Hindu trinity

Siddhartha Gautama *(B)* Historical Buddha, born in Lumbini, Nepal

Simha *(H)* Mythical lion

Sita *(H, S)* Wife of Rama; character in *Ramayana*

Skanda *(H)* God of war

Snaradroni *(H)* Part of the base holding a linga

Somasutra Stone channel used to drain off ritual ablution fluids from a sacred image

Spean *(Kh)* Bridge

Srah *(Kh)* Artificial pond

Srei *(Kh)* Woman

Stele *(Gr)* Upright stone with carved inscriptions

Stucco Plaster used as a decorative covering on walls

Stung *(Kh)* River

Stupa *(B, S)* Buddhist reliquary; shrine in the shape of a dome; Buddhist symbol of enlightenment

Sugriva *(H)* Monkey king; ally of Rama; character in *Ramayana*; dethroned by his brother Valin

Superimposition Placement of one thing on top of another; in Khmer architecture, the levels of the sanctuary tower as they gradually diminish

Surya *(H)* God of the sun; one of the three most important gods of *Rig Veda*

Symmetry Correspondence of size, shape, and arrangement of forms on either side of a dividing line

Tandava *(H)* Dance of Shiva between creation and destruction

Tantra *(B, S)* Esoteric Buddhist or Hindu ritual text; late Mahayana sect

Temple mountain Khmer stone temple in the shape of a stepped pyramid, symbolizing Mount Meru

Terrace Unroofed paved area adjacent to a building

Tevoda *(Kh)* Female divinity

Therevada *(B)* Major division of Hinayana or southern Buddhism, practiced today in Cambodia, Thailand, Laos, Myanmar, and Sri Lanka

Thma puok *(Kh)* Mudstone; Cambodian name for sandstone

Tonle Sap *(Kh)* The great lake

Trimurti *(H)* Brahmic trinity of the Hindu gods Brahma, Vishnu, and Shiva

Tympanum Triangular section of a pediment

Uma *(H)* Goddess wife of Shiva, daughter of the Himalaya; also known as Parvati, Gauri, and Devi

Urna *(B)* Halo

Vajra *(H)* Thunderbolt; attribute of the god Indra

Valin *(H)* King of the monkeys, son of Indra

Vamana *(H)* Incarnation of Vishnu as a dwarf

Varaha *(H)* Incarnation of Vishnu as a boar

Varman *(H, S)* Protector

Varuna *(H)* God of the ocean; ruler of the waters of the atmosphere and the earth; guardian of the West

Vasuki *(H)* King of the *nagas;* serpent upon which Vishnu reclines; also known as Sesa and Ananta

Vat *(Kh)* Modern Khmer Buddhist temple

Vault Arched roof, ceiling, or chamber

Veda *(H, S)* Sacred book of the Brahmans

Vihara *(H)* Rectangular building that houses a sacred image

Vihear *(Kh)* Sanctuary

Viradha *(H)* Character in *Ramayana*

Vishnu *(H, S)* Principal god of Hindu trinity; preserver and protector; maintainer of the universe

Vishvakarman *(H)* Divine architect, son of Shiva

Wat *(Th)* Modern Thai Buddhist monastery

Yaksa *(H, S)* General term for demon; giant of Lanka; character in *Ramayana*

Yaksha *(H, S)* Genie of good or evil

Yama *(H, S)* God of justice and the underworld; guardian of the south; usually depicted on a buffalo

Yoga *(H, S)* Spiritual discipline used to gain control over mind and body

Yoni *(H, S)* Womb, symbol of female genitalia; fertility

Yuga *(H, S)* One of four divisions in the Hindu world cycle

INDEX

Baphuon, 27, 39, *80*, 173, *175*, 176, 183, 184, 188, 270; conservation efforts at, 80, 176; floor plan of, *273*

barays (reservoirs), 26, 27, 28, 33, 172, 207, 260–61; East Baray, 26, 160, 173, 175; Western Baray, 7, 27, *109*, *164–65*, 172, 271

Bassac River, 257

Bat Chum, 174

bathing pools, *138–39*, 260

Battambang, 20, 28

Bayon, 7, *33–34*, 66, *92–101*, 173–74, 177–78, 179, 183, 187, 270, *back cover*; bas-reliefs at, 34, *98–100*, 177, 182, 184–85, 212; Buddhas at, *100*, 267; colossal faces at, 34, *96–97*; conservation efforts at, 189; floor plan of, *273*; Mount Meru symbolism and, 23, 33, *95*

Beng Mealea, 7, 10, 12, 37n, *191*, *192*, *232–35*, 262, 272; floor plan of, *262*

Bhavalai, 253

Bhavapura, 26, 27

block and tackle, 182

bodhisattvas, 17, 31, 32, 33, 34, *96–97*, 178

Bos Prah Nan, 267

Brahma, 24, 25, 34, 211; Angkor Wat plan and, 105, 106; depictions of, *195*, *228–30*

brahmans (Hindu priests), 16, 24, 179; backlash against, 23; *devaraja* cult and, 21, 22, 27; increased role and status of, 22

brick, 173, 175, 176, 180, 185, 186

bronze, 183, 186

Buddha, 24, 30, 31, 37n, 238; depictions of, 15, *54*, *85*, *100*, *131*, *133*, *137*, *148*, 173, 176, 187, *224–25*, 227, 245, 264, 266, 267

Buddha Dipankara, *30–31*

Buddhavamsa Jatakas, *131*

Buddhism, 11, 23, 30–31, 32, 33, 107, 188; Hindu backlash and, 23, 34; Indian influence and, 15, 16, 17, 23, 24, 30–31; Jayavarman VII's support for, 32, 173, 178; Mahayana, 27, 31, 32, 34, 35, 101, 245; *neak ta* and, 18; sacred geography of, 23; tenets of, 30, 37n; Theravada, 29, 34, 35, 36, 37n,

54, 176, 208; two main divisions of, 31

Buddhist Boundary Post, 267

Buddhist monks, 5, 9–10, 16, 18, 30, 31, 35, 37n

building materials, 180–83. *See also specific materials*

C

calendars, ritual, 60

calendrical significance, of Angkor Wat, 102–7

Cambodia: civil war in, 11, 188; climate of, 256–57, 259, 260–63; drainage axis in, 257–58; geography of, 256, 257; history of, 12–37, 186, 258–59; hydrology of, 260–61; language of, 19, 171; tourism in, 268–69

Cardamom Mountains, 256, 257

carving in situ, 184

causeways, 42, *144–45*, *150*; at Angkor Thom, 64–69; as processional routes, 171–72; symbolism of, 67, 179

ceilings, wood-coffered, 185

Central Highlands, 256

Central Plains, 256, 257

Cham, 16, 20, 29, 30, 32, *98–99*, 171, 179, 259

Champa, 16, 21, 26, 28, 30, 31, 259, 263

Chandra, 102, 105

Chau Say Tevoda, 7, *109*, *110–13*, 189, 271

Chenla, 19, 20–21, 26, 28, 31, 172, 258

Chhlong Highlands, 256

China, 15, 29, 31, 36, 257, 258; Cultural Relics Bureau of, 189

Chinese sources, 10, 16, 19–20, 28, 29, 34–35, 173, 176, 183, 186, 259, 260

Chou Ta-kuan (Zhou Daguan), 10, 28, 34–35, 173, 176, 183, 186, 259, 260

Churning of the Sea of Milk myth, 48, 53, 105, 177, 255

Citadel of Women, 218. *See also* Banteay Srei

civil war, 11, 188

clay deposits, 180

climate, 256–57, 259; *barays* and, 260–61; construction

campaigns and, 261–63

Coedès, Georges, 10, 14, 18

colossal statues, 64–65, *96–97*, *150*

columns, construction of, 183, 184

Commaille, Jean, 187

compass bearings, temple siting and, 170

consecration dates, 261–62

conservation efforts, 11, 14, 186–89

construction methods, 183–85

corbeling, 148, 183, 185

cosmography (sacred geography), 23–24, 171, 173, 261. *See also* Mount Meru

creation myths, 24, 48, 53, 105, 177, 231, 255

cruciform architectural features, 85, 121, 124, 148, 171, 177, 178

Customs of Cambodia (Chou). *See* Chou Ta-kuan

D

daily life, depictions of, 34, *100*, 177–78

Dam Deik, 180

dancers, 52, 149; *apsaras* and, 10, 25, 53, 179, 189; Preah Khan Hall of Dancers and, *148*, 178–79, 185

Dangkrek Mountains, 248, 253, 256

decoration, of temple surfaces, 186

deities, 29; in ancient Indian religious sytem, 22; Mount Meru as home of, 23, 26. *See also* Hindu deities; *specific deities*

Delaporte, Louis, 10, *103*, 262

devarajas (god-kings), 21–22, 27, 61, 171, 202

devas, 48

devatas (divinities), *18*, *112*, *117*, *124*, *130*, *148*, *155*, *158*, 177, 185, 186, *218*, 220

Dharanindravarman, 178

Dharanindravarman I, 29

Dharanindravarman II, 30

dharma, 23

Dharmaraja, 77

Divakarabhatta, 16

domestic architecture, 170, 174, 180

Dongson bronze culture, 14

doorways, sculpted stone, 82, 125, 163, 172, 174, 180, 182, 199, 220; construction of, 184; timber doors and, 185

Doudart de Lagrée, Ernest, 10

Durga, 220

Durga Mahishasuramardini, 265

Durham Cathedral, 180

dvarapalas, 129, 155, 205, 209, 218, 220

E

East Baray, 26, 160, 173, 175

East Mebon, 7, 26, 109, 160–63, 173, 174, 175–76, 271; floor plan of, 274

Ecole Française d'Extrême-Orient (EFEO), 14, 37, 176, 178, 186–88, 260

Elephant Mountains, 256

elephants, 28, 139, 170, 171, 181; depictions of, 75, 162, 220

Elephant Terrace (Angkor Thom), 39, 72–75, 188, 270

El Niño Southern Oscillation (ENSO), 256–57, 258, 263

Endeavor, 37

F

Fachhochschule, 189

Filliozat, Jean, 26

fish, 258, 259

Floating Village, 7, 191, 212–13

floor plans, 273–75

forts, 14

foundations, 184

Fournereau, Lucien, 13, 175

France: colonial rule of, 14, 186; conservation efforts and, 186–88

Funan, 15–16, 19–20, 31, 172, 258

G

gallery design, 175

gandharvas (heavenly musicians), 25

Ganesha, 24–25, 160

Ganges, 24, 226

Garnier, Francis, 10

garudas (birds), 25; depictions of, 74, 138–39, 142, 150, 151, 178, 267

Gate of Death, 39, 71, 266, 270

Gauri, 202

geography, 256, 257; sacred, 23–24, 171, 173, 261 (*see also* Mount Meru)

German Apsara Conservation Project, 189

Glaize, Maurice, 187, 192, 198

gold, 183, 186

Goodman, James, 11, 256–63

gopuras (gateways), 42, 44, 85, 113–15, 124, 137, 145–46, 155–57, 159, 168, 172, 178, 179, 183, 189, 195–97, 216, 250, 251, 255; at Angkor Thom, 64–71

Great Departure, The, 133

Great Processional Ways, 171–72

Groslier, Bernard-Philippe, 9, 10, 11, 116, 187, 260

Groslier, Georges, 10, 264

Groslier, Philippe, 187–88

Guardian with Monkey Head, 266

H

hamsa (goose), 25

Harihara, 25, 266

Hariharalaya, 21, 25, 26, 199

Harshavarman I, 270, 271

Himalaya, 226

Hindu creation myth, 24, 48, 53, 105, 177, 231, 255

Hindu deities, 22, 24–25, 34, 174; Buddhist perspective on, 30; calendrical measurements as offerings to, 104; human dignitaries combined with, 25, 32, 96, 102–4, 202, 208; local ideas and, 17, 25; plethora of temple sites devoted to, 179. *See also specific deities*

Hindu epics, 17, 24; depictions of scenes from, 2–3, 48, 80, 114–15, 177, 222, 223, 239, 245

Hinduism, 8, 11, 32, 33, 35, 107, 179, 184, 188; astronomical knowledge and, 104; backlash against, 23, 34; calendrical cycles and, 102, 106; Indian influence and, 16, 17, 22–23, 24,

172; sacred geography of, 23, 171, 173, 261; temple practices and, 179

Hindu priests. *See* brahmans

hospitals, 33, 262

Houses of the Sacred Flame, 33

hunting scenes, 75

hydrology, 170, 260–61. *See also barays*

I

ICCROM, 189

imperial power, 27–28

India, 258, 261, 263; astronomical knowledge in, 104, 106; genesis of Buddhist tradition in, 30

Indian influence, 14, 34; architecture and, 17, 170, 172, 174, 180; in Funan period, 15–16; indigenous Khmer religion and, 17–19, 22; military culture and, 28; nature of dynamic in, 16–17; religious ideas and, 16, 17, 22–25, 29, 30–31, 32, 172

Indonesian conservation efforts, 189

Indra, 22

Indratataka, 172, 207

Indravarman I, 25–26, 172, 198, 204, 207, 272

Indravarman II, 34, 270, 271

Indravarman III, 270

inscriptions: earliest in region, 19; information garnered from, 19–20, 171; as only surviving written records, 170–71; scholarship on, 14

interiors and decoration, 185–86

International Coordinating Committee for Safeguarding Angkor (ICC), 189

iron, 183

irrigation, 260, 261

Isanavarman I, 20

Issan, Thailand: Muang Tam at, 7, 191, 240–41, 272; Prasat Phimai at, 7, 191, 242–45, 272; Prasat Phnom Rung at, 7, 191, 192, 236–39, 272, 275; Prasat Sikhoraphum at, 7, 191, 246–47, 272

Italian conservation efforts, 189

naval power, 28
Neak Pean, 7, 33, 109, 152–53, 187, 260, 271
neak ta (ancestor spirits), 8, 18, 224–25, 226
nirvana, 30, 37n
North Star, 105
Notre Dame (Paris), 180
numbers, sacred, 107

O

Oc Eo, 15
Old Khmer, 19
oracle, 153

P

palace complexes, 173, 174, 177, 179
Pali, 31, 35, 37n
Pandava brothers, 24
Parmentier, Henri, 10
Parvati, 25, 160, 228–29
Phimai, 33. See Prasat Phimai
Phimeanakas, 23–24, 39, 81–82, 120, 173, 176, 183, 270, 273; floor plan of, 273; stairways at, 81, 180
Phnom Bakheng, 7, 12, 26, 58–61, 109, 171, 172–73, 270; floor plan of, 273
Phnom Bok, 173
Phnom Krom, 7, 173, 191, 210–11, 272
Phnom Kulen, 7, 21, 191, 224–27, 272
Phnom Penh, 35, 36, 257, 258
Phnom Rung. See Prasat Phnom Rung
planets, 107
plaster, 186
Polaris, 105
Po Nagar, 26
Portuguese visitors, 35, 186
post-and-lintel construction, 183
pottery sites, 174, 180, 188
pradakshinas (circular paved walkways), 95
Prasat Kravan, 7, 109, 140–43, 174, 180, 188, 271
Prasat Krol Ko, 7, 109, 155, 271
Prasat Phimai, 7, 191, 242–45, 272

Prasat Phnom Rung, 7, 191, 192, 236–39, 272; floor plan of, 275
Prasat Prei, 7, 109, 155, 271
Prasat Sikhoraphum, 7, 191, 246–47, 272
Prasat Suor Prat, 39, 88–89, 189, 270
Preah Khan (Angkor), 7, 11, 32, 33, 109, 144–51, 157, 170, 173, 178–79, 181, 182, 183, 186, 262, 267, 271; conservation efforts at, 188; floor plan of, 274; Hall of Dancers of, 148, 178–79, 185; inscriptions at, 171, 179, 183; temporary palace complex at, 179
Preah Khan (Kompong Svay), 27, 33
preah khan (sacred sword), 146, 171, 178
Preah Ko, 7, 25, 26, 172, 174, 180, 186, 202–5, 272
Preah Ko style, 172
Preah Palilay, 34, 39, 84, 270
Preah Pithu, 39, 86–87, 270
Preah Vihear, 7, 10, 191, 248–55, 267, 272; floor plan of, 275
pre-Angkorian period, 172
prehistoric culture, 14–15, 18
Prei. See Prasat Prei
Prei Veng, 265
Pre Rup, 7, 26, 109, 166–69, 173, 175, 271; floor plan of, 274
priests: astronomical knowledge of, 104–5, 107. See also brahmans
pulleys, 182
pyramidal architectural features, 25–26, 27, 33, 162, 166–69, 175, 176, 182
Pyu, 31

Q

quarrying, 181
quincunx, 173

R

Rajavihara, 33, 127
Rajendrasvara, 162
Rajendravarman I, 271, 272
Rajendravarman II, 26–27, 167, 176, 217
Rama, Prince, 24
Ramayana, 17, 24; depictions of

scenes from, 2–3, 48, 114–15, 177, 222, 223, 239, 245
Ratanakiri Plateau, 256
Ravana, 24, 219, 222
rebirth, 23, 30, 31
reservoirs. See barays
rice cultivation, 9, 20, 28, 259, 260, 261
road systems, 26, 33, 181, 262
Roluos group, 7, 172, 174, 191, 196–209, 268, 272. See also Bakong; Lolei; Preah Ko
Rong Chen, 32
roof construction, 185
royal audiences, 35
royal palaces, 173, 174, 177, 179
Ruisey, 228

S

sacrifices, 22, 24
Sailendras, 21
Sakyamuni, 32
Sambor, 258–59
Sambor Prei Kuk, 265
Sanday, John, 11, 170–89
sandstone, 119, 170, 172, 173, 174, 176, 177, 181–82, 183; carving of, 184–85; colors of, 184; construction methods and, 183–85; "paneling" applied to, 183; plaster decoration over, 186; polishing surface of, 182; quarrying of, 181, 182; transportation of, 181–82; varieties of, 182
Sanskrit, 16, 17, 18, 19, 20, 21, 35, 36, 171
Sarasvati, 25
satellite images, 257, 261
seafaring, 14
self, in Indian belief system, 23
Sesha, 24, 25
Shiva, 17, 23, 24, 25, 26, 33, 63, 101, 102, 211, 226; depictions of, 22, 168, 215, 218, 219, 221, 228–29, 246–47; shrines dedicated to, 145, 147, 160, 173, 179, 202, 209, 237, 240, 253
Siddhartha Gautama, 131, 133
Siem Reap, 258
Siem Reap Province, 268
Siem Reap River, 181, 226, 226, 228, 259, 261

ACKNOWLEDGMENTS

This undertaking, spanning many years, would not have been possible without the generous support of numerous individuals and their belief in the artistic merit of the photographs and the cultural importance of Angkor. I am deeply grateful to all of them.

Martha McGuire diligently dedicated her time and abilities, editing a huge amount of images and text, scanning and organizing the material, creating design ideas, and patiently writing captions. She was by my side on location and in the studio.

Robert Abrams provided pivotal support for the project. He appreciated and understood the photography and was willing to assemble the resources necessary to publish the book.

Susan Costello recognized the importance of the project and patiently guided it through the lengthy production process, keeping us on schedule and offering encouragement to the entire team. She clarified and improved the structure and content of the book.

Julietta Cheung undertook a complex new subject with optimism and artistic sophistication. Her design unifies the texts and illuminates the photography.

Louise Kurtz managed the important final phases of production, including the color separations.

John Sanday made time in his demanding schedule to write his important text. His expertise and insight, gained from years of work at Angkor, were invaluable.

Ian Mabbett generously expanded his piece under time constraints, interweaving his great wealth of knowledge of the history of the Khmer with a sensitive understanding of their spirituality.

Eleanor Mannikka created a synopsis of her fascinating, complex, and important research.

James Goodman shared his current research on hydrology in Cambodia.

El Kazan, Rob Ritchie, and Eric Valdman took special care in processing the color film at Time Life Photographic Labs, New York City.

My brother, Richard Ortner, and dear friend, Neal Goldsmith, were always there, to listen, comment, appreciate, and help me express my thoughts.

In Cambodia

Her Royal Highness Samdech Preak Ream Norodom Bopha Tevi kindly gave permission to photograph the collection of the National Museum of Cambodia.

Kerya Chau Sun of APSARA facilitated our permission to photograph the monuments, and graciously shared her time, advice, and friendship. Her intelligent perceptions gave us a greater understanding of the complexities of Cambodia and the future of Angkor.

The Sou Ny family has warmly welcomed us into their home, the charming Angkorianna Villa in Siem Reap, for many long stays. Vuoch Lim nurtured us and watched after our every need with loving care.

Mrs. Tep Vatho of APSARA understood our goals and the importance of the project and helped move it forward. Her husband, Mr. Oliviea, proprietor of the Angkor Village Hotel, kindly provided elephants and mahouts.

Ouk Lay, the minister of culture and fine arts, patiently arranged permission for our photography at the Cambodian National Museum.

Khun Samen and Hab Touch gracefully facilitated the photography at the Cambodian National Museum.

Our two able driver/guides, Mr. Soy and Leang Chhay, were unfailingly punctual and cheerful during months of rigorous photography that required the hauling of heavy equipment, complex translations, and negotiation of the challenging road conditions in rural Cambodia.

Madam Boran Kim, director of the Wat Bo Dancers, and Madam Rosa Khun brought their troupes to the temple sites at dawn, transporting costumes, fresh flowers, makeup artists, and music. The dancers performed with elegance, grace, and enthusiasm.

Alice Harvey arranged the dance photography at Preah Khan.

Pascal Ronepe of EFEO, construction manager at Baphuon, graciously allowed photography during the ongoing renovation.

The management and staff of Thai Airways International were unfailingly efficient, and helpful in transporting equipment, allowing overweight baggage, and politely hand checking and making room for film onboard the aircraft.

Editor: Susan Costello
General Consultant: John Sanday
Copyeditors: Miranda Ottewell, Marian Appellof
Art Director, Designer, and Schematic Maps:
Julietta Cheung, Freeform Studio, Inc.
Production Manager: Louise Kurtz

First Edition
10   9   8   7   6   5   4   3   2   1

Library of Congress Cataloging-in-Publication Data

Ortner, Jon, 1951-
Angkor : celestial temples of the Khmer empire / photographs by Jon Ortner ; text by
Ian Mabbett ... [et al.].— 1st ed.
p. cm.
Includes index.
ISBN 0-7892-0718-4 (alk. paper)
1. Angkor (Extinct city) 2. Angkor (Extinct city)—Pictorial works.
3. Temples—Cambodia—Angkor (Extinct city)
4. Temples—Cambodia—Angkor (Extinct city)—Pictorial works.
1. Mabbett, Ian W. 11. Title.

DS554.98.A5 O77 2006
959.6'03 — dc21
2002141551

ABOUT THE PHOTOGRAPHER

Jon Ortner and Martha McGuire

Jon Ortner has been based in New York City since 1978 where he has created images for notable architectural and commercial clients. His great passion has been photographing Hindu and Buddhist monuments and traditions in the Himalaya and Southeast Asia. His images have appeared in several books including Abbeville's *Sacred Places of Asia: Where Every Breath Is a Prayer* and *Manhattan Dawn and Dusk*.

ABOUT THE AUTHORS

John Sanday, who served as the general consultant for this book and contributed the essay on architecture and conservation, is a conservation architect and has been the World Monuments Fund Field Director in Cambodia since 1989.

Ian Mabbett, an authority on Indian states and cultures, studied Sanskrit at Oxford and teaches at Monash University in Melbourne. He is the co-author of *The Khmers*.

Eleanor Mannikka is the author of *Angkor Wat: Time, Space and Kingship* about the calendrical significance of Angkor Wat.

James Goodman heads an architectural and engineering firm in Kathmandu specializing in the conservation of historic buildings and monuments. He has been researching the hydrology of Angkor for the last five years.

Kerya Chau Sun is a director at the APSARA Authority, which controls the tourist development of the monuments at Angkor.

ALSO AVAILABLE FROM
ABBEVILLE PRESS

Borobudur
Text by Louis Frédéric   Photography by Jean-Louis Nou
ISBN 0-7892-0134-8

Sacred Places of Asia:
Where Every Breath Is a Prayer
By Jon Ortner   Preface by John Sanday
ISBN 0-7892-0705-2

ABBEVILLE PRESS
116 West 23rd Street, New York, New York 10011
1-800-ARTBOOK (in U.S. only)
Available wherever fine books are sold

ISBN 0-7892-0718-4

Printed in China

Visit us at
www.abbeville.com